cook's practical handbook:

ice cream

cook's practical handbook:

ice cream

an enticing guide to making ice creams and iced desserts

sara lewis

LORENZ BOOKS

This edition is published by Lorenz Books

Lorenz Books is an imprint of Anness Publishing Ltd
Hermes House, 88–89 Blackfriars Road, London SE1 8HA
tel. 020 7401 2077; fax 020 7633 9499;
www.lorenzbooks.com; info@anness.com

This edition distributed in the UK by Aurum Press Ltd,
25 Bedford Avenue, London WC1B 3AT
tel. 020 7637 3225; fax 020 7580 2469

This edition distributed in the USA and Canada by National
Book Network, 4720 Boston Way, Lanham, MD 20706
tel. 301 459 3366; fax 301 459 1705; www.nbnbooks.com

This edition distributed in Australia by Pan Macmillan Australia,
Level 18, St Martins Tower, 31 Market St, Sydney, NSW 2000
tel. 1300 135 113; fax 1300 135 103; email
customer.service@macmillan.com.au

This edition distributed in New Zealand by David Bateman Ltd,
30 Tarndale Grove, Off Bush Road, Albany, Auckland
tel. (09) 415 7664; fax (09) 415 8892

Previously published as part of a larger compendium, *Ice Cream and Iced
Desserts*

PUBLISHER: Joanna Lorenz
MANAGING EDITOR: Linda Fraser
SENIOR EDITOR: Margaret Malone
DESIGNER: Luise Roberts
PHOTOGRAPHY: Gus Filgate (recipes), Craig Robertson
(equipment, techniques, steps and still lifes)
FOOD FOR PHOTOGRAPHY: Joanna Farrow (recipes), Annabel Ford
(equipment, techniques, and steps)
STYLING: Penny Markham

NOTES

For all recipes, quantities are given in both metric and imperial measures and,
where appropriate, measures are also given in standard cups and spoons. Follow
one set, but not a mixture, because they are not interchangeable.

Standard spoon and cup measures are level.
1 tsp = 5ml, 1 tbsp = 15ml, 1 cup = 250ml/8fl oz

Australian standard tablespoons are 20ml. Australian readers should use 3
tsp in place of 1 tbsp for measuring small quantities of gelatine,
cornflour, salt, etc.

Medium eggs are used unless otherwise stated.

10 9 8 7 6 5 4 3 2 1

contents

The World of Ice Cream

Ice cream must be one of the few dishes in the world that is loved by virtually everyone, from the young to the young at heart, and the out-and-out foodie, searching for the ultimate flavour combination, to the devotee with more traditional tastes and a preference for timeless and classic favourites.

AN ADAPTABLE TREAT

With ice cream, there really is something for everyone. From the easiest of creations – the simple ice cream cone – to more elaborate terrines and moulded ice desserts, ice cream and ices have proved, since their inception, to be quite irresistible. On a hot summer's day nothing better evokes childhood pleasure than a creamy Tutti Frutti or crunchy Rocky Road ice cream, whilst refreshing fruit sorbets and snow-like granitas are ideal for serving between courses to cleanse the palate, after an elegant supper or relaxed *al fresco* meal.

Within this comprehensive guide are all the best and well-loved ice creams, water ices, sorbets and granitas. You'll find all the classics, plus more adventurous mixtures that prove just how exciting ice creams can be. Some of the recipes are highly indulgent, but there are also low-fat treats for those on special diets, or who are trying to control their calorie intake.

We explore the history and early developments of this fascinating food, take you on a cook's tour of specialities from all around the world, and unravel the differences between sherbet and water ice, sorbet and semi-freddo, gelato and granita. We guide you through the maze of ingredients, flavourings, equipment and techniques, and bring you detailed, easy-to-follow photographed steps, so that even the most inexperienced cook will feel sure about attempting every recipe, however complicated.

ABOVE: *Made with simple ingredients, sorbet is a light and delicious dessert.*

PROFESSIONAL TIPS

There are lots of helpful tips for successful ices with or without an ice cream maker, and advice on the best way to store iced desserts after you have made them. The detailed reference section shows how to transform a basic ice cream into a more sumptuous dessert through the use of moulds, baskets and ice bowls. Recipes are provided for all the classic sauces, such as Melba and Butterscotch. Tips for toppings and decorative techniques give further ideas for ways of serving ice cream.

THE FLAVOURS OF HOMEMADE ICE CREAM

For anyone lucky enough to taste homemade ice cream the difference between it and many commercially made brands is immediate. The simple use of a few good quality basic ingredients and flavourings makes all the difference. Divided into four chapters, the recipes explore all the classic combinations and flavourings from around the world.

Starting at the beginning, the first chapter contains the best sorbets, granitas and water ices. Traditionally served between courses, sorbets and granitas range from the classically smooth and tangy Lemon Sorbet to the vibrant flavour of Coffee Granita. In the second chapter, however, resides the real heart of ice cream – it contains the best vanilla, chocolate and coffee ice creams – and you will find them hard to resist. Recipes such as Dark Chocolate and Hazelnut Praline, crunchy Cookies and Cream and smooth Coffee Toffee Swirl, are simple, delicious and also look superb.

Fruit and nut ice creams come next, and show how imaginative use of seasonal fruit and a few chopped nuts can transform a basic ice cream into a special treat. The last chapter contains some surprising and tasty cream-free and low-fat ices.

AN INTERNATIONAL FLAVOUR

The range of recipes includes ice creams and water ices from the Middle East, India, the British Isles and the Americas. Unusual ingredients include sweeteners, such as honey or maple syrup, using yogurt instead of cream, and the addition of flower essences, herbs, nuts and even spices.

Ice cream is no longer a symbol of wealth, but is one of life's affordable luxuries. Universally acknowledged as one of the best loved comfort foods, it gives you a lift when you need it, and many problems have been solved – or friendships forged – over a tub of chocolate ripple or rocky road. Of course, ice cream can be mass produced, with cheaper ingredients than any you'll find in this book, but there is really no substitute for the real thing in all its calorie-laden glory.

ABOVE: *A welcome refresher from the heat, ice cream is sold at an ice cream parlour near Broken Hill in New South Wales, Australia.*

ABOVE: *Although ice cream making started off slowly in Italy, it soon developed and Italian ice creams have enjoyed worldwide popularity ever since.*

EARLY HISTORY OF ICE

It is known that ice houses were built around four thousand years ago at Mari, beside the river Euphrates, in Mesopotamia. These were apparently used for cooling wine and it is likely that chilled wines and fruit juices were the precursors of our modern-day ice cream.

By the beginning of the 1st century AD, there is some evidence that snow and ice were being appreciated for themselves, and not just as a means for cooling other ingredients. The Roman emperor Nero Claudius Caesar is reputed to have sent his slaves into the mountains to gather fresh snow, which was dressed with honey and fruits, for a special feast.

Such uses for snow and ice appear to have been rare, however. By the time of the 5th century, there is evidence that snow was sold in the markets of Athens, but this would undoubtedly have been far too dirty and full of debris to have been used for more than cooling drinks and possibly for short term preservation of food.

The Mameluke kings of Egypt had snow shipped from Lebanon to Cairo in the 13th and 14th centuries, while in Spain there is evidence that snow pits were used from 1387 onwards. These early European ice houses

ABOVE: *Despite the wintery weather, a young child enjoys ice cream near Winnipeg, Manitoba.*

were simple unlined pits. Although primitive in construction, they worked quite well, because the constant temperature maintained below ground is such a good insulator. There is record of an Italian ice trade which began on a small scale in the 15th century and developed into a system of hauling ice by horse-drawn wagon to the major cities of northern Italy. At this stage, ice was still used largely as a coolant, it was ideal for chilling drinks and food but ineffective when it came to actually freezing liquids.

THE FIRST ICED DESSERTS

No one knows for certain who produced the world's first ice cream although it is probable that it was the Chinese who first developed the art of making iced desserts. They are known to have chilled fruit juices and tea, which led to their making primitive fruit-flavoured ices some two thousand years ago. When Marco Polo returned from the East in the 13th century, he told of an iced drink which consisted of a sweet, syrupy flower essence, paste or powder, which was diluted with water, then chilled with ice or snow. The drink was called "chorbet" in Turkish and "charab" in Persian and although it was never actually frozen, it evolved to become sorbet, the frozen dessert we know today.

A SCIENTIFIC ADVANCE

In 1620 scientists and chemists working with nitre (potassium nitrate and sodium nitrate) discovered that it was possible to use it to liquefy ice and snow, and in so doing to reduce the temperature below freezing point. This endothermic effect could also be achieved using common salt (sodium chloride) and when a mixture of ice and salt was packed around a container of water, the water turned to ice. This had many implications including the potential for making iced desserts.

Ices for the Elite

During the seventeenth and eighteenth centuries, fashionable society throughout Europe enjoyed elegance and opulence in all things. The style of clothes, interiors and entertaining was rich and sumptuous and spectacular iced desserts became an essential addition to the menu on any grand occasion.

EARLY WATER ICES

As more efficient ways of freezing were developed, the technique of making ices rapidly developed into an art form and a status symbol for the very rich. As scientists and scholars across Europe continued to study the laws behind freezing water, given further impetus by the invention of the thermometer in the 18th century, others turned this knowledge into creating objects of beauty.

There is evidence that water ices were made in Italy in the 1550s, and when Marie de Medici married Henry IV of France in the late 16th century, she introduced the French court to "sorbetti"; the banqueting tables were soon glittering with beautiful ice pyramids. These sorbetti – or sorbets – were quite different from the ones served today. Made with an alcoholic base, they were eaten between savoury main courses, and also substituted for liqueurs at grand banquets. Making them was highly skilled work, which was carried out by a "liqueriste". The most renowned of these were L. Audiger, a professional confectioner and distiller of liqueurs and aromatic waters to the young Louis XIV in the 1660s, and Massialot, who featured recipes for chocolate water ice and custard ice in his cookbook, which was published in 1692. It is interesting to note that these early ice creams were sometimes referred to as "cheeses", possibly because they were usually made in the dairy.

Fruit flavours predominated in these early sorbets, but flower waters such as jasmine, violet, tuberose, orange blossom and jonquil were also used, as were infusions of green fennel, burnet and chervil.

ABOVE: *A coloured engraving showing fashionable ladies choosing ice cream,*

MASSIALOT'S FROMAGE A L'ANGLOISE

"Take 16oz of sweet cream and the same of milk, ¹/₂lb powdered [icing] sugar, stir in 3 egg yolks and boil it until it becomes a thin pap. Take it from the fire and pour it into your ice mould and put it on ice for 3 hours. When it is firm, withdraw the mould and warm it a little in order more easily to turn out your cheese, or else dip your mould for a moment in hot water, then serve in a compotier."

This recipe from Massialot's book The Court and Country Cook *was reprinted in Elizabeth David's book,* Harvest of the Cold Months, *Michael Joseph 1994.*

RIGHT: *A Sevres dessert service was only for the very wealthy. It includes a* plat de ménage, *dish, cup and saucer and large ice cream bowl. From the Blue Cameo Service, Sevres, 1778–9. Part of a collection belonging to the Hermitage,*

9kg | 20lbs of ice mixed with 450g | 1lb salt, and it is also interesting to note that there are no eggs in many of the recipes. The ice cream is frozen without using a churn, so would have tasted quite different from our modern ice creams. It wasn't until later in the 18th century that the French introduced eggs and cream cheeses to ice creams, making them much richer.

A few years after Mary Eales published her book, in 1722 Mary Smith included ten iced desserts in her publication *The Complete House-Keeper and Professed Cook*. These included Brown Bread Ice Cream, which is often thought of as a modern invention. Also on the list were Italian Ice Cream, Raspberry Cream, Orange Cream, Peach Cream and Apricot Cream. Some were cream-based and others were water ices, but as at this stage ice creams did not include eggs they were, literally, iced creams.

IMPROVEMENTS IN TASTE AND TEXTURE

During the 18th century, it was recognized that a superior ice cream could be made if the mixture was churned until it was thick and semi-frozen, then spooned into a mould for a second freezing. Ice cream made by this method had a creamier, smoother texture than that of earlier ice cream desserts, and the ice crystals were much finer.

Flavourings become much more adventurous, too, and varied from exotic fruits such as bananas and pineapples to fresh berry fruit, preserves, chestnut, cinnamon and white coffee cream. Other flavourings included Italian cream with cinnamon, lemon, brandy and the nut liqueur, noyau. One of the more bizarre offerings included lightly poached cucumber, ginger, brandy, coffee and cream. By 1885, modern cooks were publishing books on making ice cream, cookery schools included the art of making iced desserts and hand-cranked ice cream makers became available.

Britain was slow to follow this new European fashion. Ice houses were not introduced until the beginning of the 17th century, and it was not until 1675 that there was the first recorded instance of ice cream being served, when King Charles ll tucked into strawberries and ice cream at a grand banquet. Interest in iced desserts grew during the reign of William and Mary, and by the time Queen Anne ascended the throne in 1702, they were extremely popular.

In Regency Britain, elegance and extravagance were all important, and London society was the heart of the British Empire. During the reign of George lll and later the Prince Regent, ice creams became extremely fashionable. Iced desserts were spectacular scented and moulded creations, set in complicated hinged moulds and served at grand balls, or conveyed to elaborate summer picnics by teams of servants bearing small portable "ice caves" or cool cabinets. Although very grand in appearance, it must be remembered that these iced desserts were not beaten during freezing, so would have been very icy to eat.

EARLY RECIPES

Mary Eales, Confectioner to the Queen, recorded some of these early recipes, first published in her book, *Mrs Eales's Receipts* in 1718, some years after she supplied ice creams to the royal court. The recipes call for very large quantities of ice to freeze these simple ice creams – as much as

From Ice Houses to Refrigerators

No discussion on ice cream would be complete without mention of the ice houses which were needed to produce a ready supply of ice in summer as well as winter. Ice houses were first introduced in the 17th century, and rapidly became status symbols in Europe.

DESIGN FEATURES

Not all ice houses proved successful. Early ice houses were simple structures covered with thatched roofs and covered with earth and shrubs for added insulation, so that only the entrances were visible. Some were badly drained, and others were built below the water table, so the mud-lined structures simply filled with water. By the mid 19th century, ice house construction had greatly improved and became enduring structures with vaulted brick roofs. Those built outside were usually entered through a north-facing door, which led down to a narrow passage divided by two or more doors, sometimes edged with leather or sheepskin for extra insulation. The passage led to a deep chamber, usually built with brick and between 2.4m | 8ft and 10m | 33ft wide. Some of the larger chambers had circular walkways; some even had brick steps down into the pit to allow easier access, although ladders were generally used to get down to the ice. Most brick-built ice houses had a chute in the roof to

make it easier to fill them with ice, which was cut from frozen lakes or ponds in the winter and transported as quickly as possible. Most large estates would have had at least one ice house. These were often quite elaborate, especially if the landowner was particularly proud of his acquisition. Some of the more ostentatious owners added decorative stone arches and columns to the entrances of their ice houses. Although most ice houses were round, square ones were also built, and some of the very elaborate ones even had dovecotes in the roofs. In some cases, the ice house was combined with the game store or linked to the banqueting house. Some of the larger town houses also had ice stores, which were built in their basements.

HARVESTING THE ICE

For ease of harvesting, ice houses were usually constructed near a lake or river, or by the side of a man-made pond known as the "freezing pond".

A team of estate workers would cut the ice with the help of long spiked poles, or by bouncing a long stretch of heavy chain across it until it broke. The ice would then be broken up, loaded into a cart and taken to the ice house, where it would be packed in tight layers in the pit. The method of packing varied from estate to estate. In some cases, the ice was packed alternately with straw; in others it was packed with a little salt and additional water. The top layer was then covered with a thick layer of straw or sawdust. Great care was taken to keep the ice as clean as possible, although it must still have been flecked with twigs and leaves.

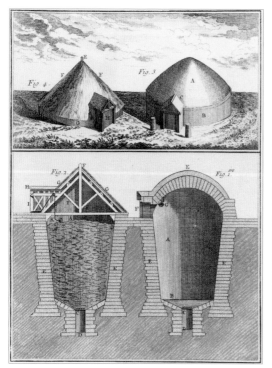

ABOVE: *Illustration of two common ice houses. The one on the left has a thatched roof, whereas the one on the right has a vaulted roof that is made of brick.*

ABOVE: *Cutting out ice that has been stored in the ice house. Workers used long spiked poles for breaking up the ice and removing it from its straw packing.*

STORING THE ICE

Food was never stored in ice houses. They were used solely for the ice itself, which was transported to the house by the wheelbarrow load, where it was washed and used in the cellars or ice storage cabinets. If the ice had been made from pure water, it could be used for desserts and drinks. If not, it would have been crushed and mixed with ammonium chloride, sodium chloride (common salt) or potassium nitrate to reduce the freezing point before being spooned into decorated china ice pails or two-tiered dishes for the serving of ice cream. The lower or outer dish would hold the ice mixture, while the ice cream would be placed in an inner dish or on the top tier.

A NEW AGE

The ice house was very popular on the large estates in Britain, but it was in America that it was refined and developed. The exclusivity which was so much a part of its history in Britain and Europe did not survive long in the United States, especially after the invention of small, cheaply built ice houses which could be built above ground. This invention made its way to Britain, and, with the lifting of printing restrictions in the 1840s, printed plans of ice houses became freely available. Ice houses were now within the reach of the suburban middle classes as well as their wealthiest contemporaries.

The transport revolution meant that ice could be shipped from America and Norway to Europe. In 1894, 400,000 tons of ice was exported from America to the UK despite the considerable cost per ton. The ever increasing railway network throughout Europe made it possible for ice to be supplied from large urban depots to country houses.

Domestic ice stores were also introduced, enabling ice to be kept in the house for several days. These basic ice cupboards, known as ice safes or ice preservers, were the forerunners of our modern refrigerators and freezers. These wooden cupboards were generally zinc or aluminium-lined with a

ABOVE: *With the introduction of mechanized ice churners, such as these wooden pails with metal canisters inside, ice cream could be produced and sold on a large scale by enterprising street sellers.*

reservoir for water and ice and would be used for keeping butter, milk and other foods cold. Ice was generally bought from the ice man who ran a home delivery service, usually once a week, and the ice would keep foods cold for several days if mixed with salt. Ice cream would need to be made on the day of the ice delivery as the ice store was little more than the modern insulated cool box.

The Americans took ice to India by ship in the 1830s, and although storage in India proved a problem at first, by the 1870s the ice trade was well established. Ice was stored in domestic mahogany or teak chests lined with zinc or slate. The wealthy British soon took to this kitchen aid and the ice chest became an indispensable household item.

THE FIRST ICE CREAM MACHINES

Very early ice cream makers consisted of small earthenware or metal pots filled with milk or cream mixtures, and placed inside deep urns or cabinets lined with either wood or lead, and surrounded with ice, ice and straw or ice and salt.

By the middle of the 19th century mechanized ice cream makers were introduced. These looked like wooden pails, with a small metal canister inside for the ice cream. The pail was filled with an ice and salt mixture and the ice cream was churned with a hand-stirrer.

LEFT: *Illustration of an early ice cream machine using a hand-cranking device for churning the ice cream.*

Early American ice cream machines worked by packing the ice cream mixture into a small pot which was shaken up and down in a wooden pail packed with ice and salt. The most famous hand-cranked ice cream maker was invented in 1843, by Nancy Johnson, a naval officer's wife in America. Later that century, in England, Agnes Marshall also developed a hand-cranked ice cream machine.

THE ITALIAN CONNECTION

Italy had always been famous for its superior ice creams but it was not until the late 19th century that Britain and America discovered the joy of Italian ice cream. This came about when political upheaval in Italy led to a huge exodus of young Italians, many of whom set up as ice cream makers in the countries that gave them refuge, often in makeshift premises on the dockside.

In the early days, ice cream street sellers were a cross between a wandering musician and street hawker. Their organ music first attracted customers to their barrows which could be quite simple affairs or highly decorated and colourful carts. Early carts were reported to have been made in the shape of a gondola. As ice cream grew in popularity, so the numbers of street sellers increased and by the turn of the century, 900 ice cream barrows were registered in Clerkenwell, London, alone.

With the growth in the number of street sellers, fighting broke out as sellers vied for the best pitches. Much of the ice cream produced was manufactured in slum conditions in domestic kitchens. Milk was boiled the previous night then frozen with ice the next day. The dishes used to serve the ice cream, known as penny licks, were simply reused and never washed. The inevitable outcome was the spread of bacterial infections, and the transfer of disease, particularly tuberculosis, became widespread. As a result of a lobby to ban the sale of ice cream, manufacturing moved to hygienic business premises and barrows were licensed to sell ice cream at specific points. This resolved the hygiene problem and restored peaceful trading. Finally, with the introduction of the edible ice cream cone in 1905, ice cream sellers became respectable once again.

Many more Italian immigrants came to Britain and America after war ended in Europe in the 1940s, in a bid to rebuild shattered lives and homes. Family-run cafes, milk bars and ice cream parlours and factories were quickly set up by the new immigrants, and Italian bakers lost no time in switching from biscuit making to making ice cream cones and wafers to meet the demands of the growing popularity of ice cream.

CENTRE: *As ice cream vendors prospered, some stalls became very elaborate, fixed structures.*

ABOVE AND LEFT: *Many early hand carts were replaced by horsedrawn carts and these, in time, became the ice cream vans familiar today.*

LARGE-SCALE PRODUCTION

The world's first ice cream plant opened in America in 1851. It was founded by Jacob Fussell, a Baltimore milk dealer, who wanted to find a new market for cream during the summer months when the supply of cream peaked. As a milk dealer, he had an advantage over his rivals, and by undercutting their prices his ice cream soon became so successful that by 1864 he had opened ice cream factories in Washington, Boston and New York.

In November 1909 the American trade journal *"Ice and Refrigeration"* featured a piece from a report written by the United States Consul in Canton, China, describing the crowds that gathered around the city's street vendors. Rather than taking out ready-frozen ice cream, the vendors were making it *in situ* with ingenious ice cream machines. Although the use of ice wasn't new to the Chinese, the style of ice cream was very different. By the 1930s, China's first American-style ice cream factory opened, and Peking sales soon reached a staggering 1,000 tons a year.

ABOVE: *Ice cream factory in Holstich, Germany 1895.*

In Russia, the first ice cream factory was built in the 1920s by Anastas Mikoyan, and the people of the former Soviet Union enjoyed ice cream at any opportunity. To Western tastes, it may seem rather odd to eat ice cream in extreme winter temperatures, but this was one of the few permitted luxuries and as such greatly enjoyed whatever the weather.

By the 1920s England was also producing ice cream on a large scale, first by the famous Wall's company and a year later by the Lyons group best known for its triple flavoured Neapolitan ice cream and the Lyons Corner Houses in London. Originally known for his meat pies, Thomas Wall first introduced ice cream manufacture into the business as a way of improving summer profits. At first ice cream production was small and made with sophisticated American production techniques. The ice cream was shaped and frozen in small brickettes, each one hand-wrapped in paper and sold by street sellers riding tricycles featuring a "stop me and buy one" sign. As popularity and production grew, so the company expanded from just one ice cream factory in Acton with seven street sellers in the 1920s to 136 depots and 8,500 tricycles by 1939.

With the outbreak of the Second World War, Wall's ice cream production stopped as food rationing was introduced. Many European factories also closed and soon the American armed forces became the biggest manufacturers of ice cream in the world.

Americans still have perhaps the greatest love of ice cream of all countries and consume 21 litres | 37 pints per person per year, compared to just 8 litres | 14 pints per person in England.

ELECTRIC DEEP FREEZERS

Early mechanical refrigerators didn't appear until the beginning of the 20th century and followed the development of the steam driven motor and later the electric motor. The very first electric refrigerator was a Domelre, made in America in 1913. A later version, the Kelvinator model, made in Detroit in 1914, soon came on the market, but both were noisy and extremely expensive. Not surprisingly most Americans preferred the cheaper wooden insulated cabinets or chests which they cooled with regular ice supplies.

In 1922 Baltzar von Platen and Carl Munters, two young engineering students in Stockholm, developed a cooling machine which could convert heat to cold by absorption. It could be driven by electricity, gas or kerosene. Initially called the D fridge, it was marketed by Electrolux in

MAKING ICE CREAM AT HOME

With the increased availability of affordable ingredients and improvements to ice cream makers, middle class housewives sought the advice of highly skilled cooks, such as Mrs Agnes B. Marshall and Mrs Beeton. In 1885 Agnes Marshall published her first book, in which she included detailed advice on making a range of ice creams, such as "cheap", "ordinary" and "common" ice cream. Her "cheap ice cream" was made using 1 pint [600ml | 2½ cups] of cream, 8 egg yolks and ¼lb [115g | 4oz | ½ cup] of sugar. Next came her "ordinary ice cream", in which the cream was replaced with milk. Her "common ice cream" was made with the same quantity of milk and sugar, but only two whisked eggs, while the "ordinary ice cream" dispensed with eggs altogether, and thickened the sweetened milk with arrowroot (15g | ½oz | 2 tbsp).

ABOVE: *An ice cream mould.*

RIGHT: *An early hand-cranked ice cream machine.*

RIGHT: *Illustration from* Süsse Speisen und Eisbomben, *published in Germany in 1907, showing a variety of iced confections.*

1925. As technology advanced so prices came down, and by 1935 the early air-cooled refrigerators were within the reach of many households. Although gaining in popularity and availability in America, the British were more cautious. Frigidaire first tried marketing refrigerators in Britain in 1924 but they remained a luxury item for the very rich until after the Second World War. It must also be remembered that supplies of electricity were unreliable and expensive and usually only available in the homes of the wealthy; working people had to rely on gas.

The chilled and frozen food industry originated in America when Clarence Birdseye revolutionized shopping and the preparation of food for the American and British housewives by going into partnership with the English ice cream manufacturer, Thomas Wall. By 1960, half the population of England had access to a domestic refrigerator, and by the 1970s, many homes owned a deep freezer, making the storage of bought and home-made ice cream possible.

A Surfeit of Choice

Ice cream has come a long way since the first ice cream parlour opened in 1776. Swirled, layered and mixed, in almost every conceivable flavour, ices are now available to suit every occasion, taste and preference, from low-fat sorbets to rich dairy premium ice cream, and sold in any quantity from a single cone to a half-gallon tub.

THE ICE CREAM CONE

It was a young Italian immigrant to America, Italo Marchiony, who first came up with the idea of an edible container for ice cream. When he started selling his ice creams and sorbets on Wall Street in New York, he spooned them into glasses. These were cumbersome and wasteful, so he started making shaped cups from waffle mixture. The cups proved very popular and he patented them in 1902. Two years later, he patented an ice cream cone, although the credit for this innovation is often given to a Syrian, Ernest A. Hamwi. According to the story, Mr Hamwi was selling waffles at the World's Trade Fair in St Louis in 1904 when a neighbouring ice cream seller sold out of dishes. He persuaded Mr Hamwi to roll one of his waffles to a cone, let it cool and filled it with his ice cream.

Made with a mixture of flour, milk and sugar, the ice cream cone quickly became popular. To help prevent breakages and spillages, a ring of non-crushable biscuit was also moulded to the top of the cone, making it ideal for small children as it caught any drips of melting ice cream.

The British traders of the 1920s were reluctant to sell these large imported cones as they were more costly and needed a greater quantity of ice cream to fill them. They preferred to sell ice cream brickettes sandwiched between much cheaper rectangular wafer biscuits. In the 1930s a box of 1200 wafers were very cheap to produce, making it possible to sell ice creams for 1 penny. However, by 1935 waffles for ice cream were introduced to supersede wafers; with the rather unusual advertising line of "Have a waffle in the cinema". Sales of wafers continued until the 1950s, until soft ice cream and the famous "99" ice cream was introduced, complete with its much loved chocolate flake bar.

ABOVE: *With the rise in the number of street sellers, ice cream was now becoming a more available treat for all. No longer sold in unhygienic glass dishes, but in small hand-wrapped brickettes, they were sold in Britain from the famous "stop me and buy one" Wall's tricycle.*

THE ICE CREAM SUNDAE

In late 19th century America, druggists (chemists) made and sold soda water in drug stores throughout the country. Flavoured with fruit syrups and whipped cream, these drinks were popular with young and old. In 1874 Robert Green of Philadelphia ran out of cream when making sodas for the 50th anniversary of the Franklin Institute. He substituted ice cream, much to the delight of the guests.

The ice cream soda soon became very popular, but you couldn't buy one on a Sunday. This was because many people believed soda water to be alcoholic, even though it was nothing of the kind, and drinking it was regarded as improper, particularly on Sundays. An ingenious drugstore concessionaire got around the ban by serving the ice cream and syrup without the soda water. He called it Ice Cream Sunday. The name was later changed to Sundae, which was judged more seemly.

LEFT: *Ice cream cornets, now called cones, are given free to children in London, UK, to celebrate Coronation Day in 1937.*

ICE CREAM PARLOURS

The first ice cream parlour is reputed to have been opened in New York City in 1776, but the business really boomed during the prohibition years. Bar owners had always served ice cream in the summer months, and when prohibition came in 1920, the more enterprising among them saw that swapping ice cream for hard liquor was one way of staying in business. By 1930, ice cream parlours were very much a part of the American scene. To stay competitive, manufacturers developed new flavours and shapes of ice cream. Eskimo pie and popsicles – or ice lollies, as they are now known – became popular.

MODERN DEVELOPMENTS

The majority of homes in America and Europe now have a refrigerator and a deep freeze, and many of us add a tub of ice cream to our weekly shopping trolley as a regular item. Not only is ice cream available in a wide range of flavours, with prices varying from the budget family-sized tub of strawberry, up to the most expensive and decadent chocolate combinations, but it is also easier now than ever before to make ice cream at home with electrical labour-saving gadgets that make tasks such as beating frozen ice cream quite effortless.

ABOVE: *An ice cream parlour, popular in the US since the prohibition when enterprising brewers converted their liquor bars to milk bars and served chilled ice cream sodas and thick creamy milk shakes instead.*

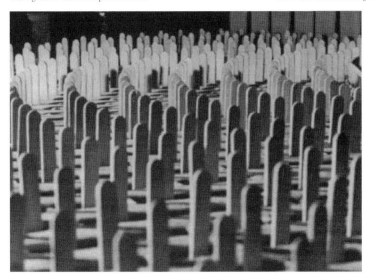

ABOVE: *The 1 penny wafer of the 1930s, and later the larger American ice cream cones, quickly grew in popularity for the young and the "young at heart".*

LEFT: *Lolly sticks at a factory in Lyon, France, 1963.*

Ice cream is loved the world over, and although it will always remain a seaside treat, it is now also seen as an everyday luxury. Probably consumed in the greatest quantities by the Americans, it is also enjoyed across Europe and India; even in the Russian winter they enjoy ice cream bought from street kiosks when there is snow on the ground!

Ways of serving ice cream have also changed dramatically over the centuries. While there is still a place for refreshing and fruity sorbets and water ices, rich creamy dairy ice creams still remain top of all opinion polls. Meanwhile, food trends have moved away from the multi-coloured, pile it high, knickerbocker glory style ice cream sundae of the 1950s or the 60s' banana split, and contemporary tastes now favour simpler, softly scooped ice creams with more imaginative but subtle flavours.

From such elitist beginnings it would have been hard to imagine that by the beginning of the 21st century there would be 500 commercially prepared ice creams available, ranging from the classic vanilla, chocolate and fruit flavours to the more exotic and eccentric such as peanut butter, lobster or tomato soup.

Dedicated ice cream cafes, parlours and franchised scoop shops now flourish in all the world's major cities. Ice cream is swirled, rippled, layered and mixed; you can buy low-fat ice cream, kosher ice cream, yogurt ice cream and a huge range of sorbets in every shape and size, from tiny individual pots and on sticks, to half-gallon tubs.

Efficient ice cream makers are now affordable, so more and more people are discovering the delights of making their own ice cream at home. This book aims to teach you to do just that, and also offers suggestions for incorporating your own favourite flavours and toppings to create wonderful desserts to suit your own tastes.

Ice cream, however simple or elaborate, should be full of natural taste and body. If you make it with the very best of ingredients, you will always enjoy the most delicious home-made ice cream.

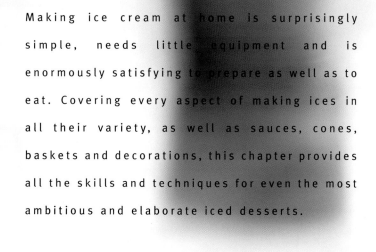

making
ice cream

Making ice cream at home is surprisingly simple, needs little equipment and is enormously satisfying to prepare as well as to eat. Covering every aspect of making ices in all their variety, as well as sauces, cones, baskets and decorations, this chapter provides all the skills and techniques for even the most ambitious and elaborate iced desserts.

Essential Equipment

You will probably already have most of the equipment you need to make successful ice creams and water ices.
Ices made by hand can simply be frozen in a plastic tub or box in the freezer, although very keen ice cream
enthusiasts may want to invest in a free-standing electric machine.

BASIC EQUIPMENT FOR MAKING ICES

Making ices by hand is the simplest method of all, and is known as "still freezing". All that you need are glass bowls and a fork, a manual or electric hand-held whisk for beating and a freezerproof container with a lid. You will also need a heavy-based saucepan for making the custard, sugar syrups and cooking fruits, plus a sieve for puréeing and a lemon squeezer and fine grater for citrus fruits.

A food processor is a useful aid for breaking down the ice crystals, although it can be wasteful of ingredients; however, this labour saving method does produce a similar texture to that made in an electric ice cream maker.

For storage

You will need a selection of freezerproof containers in varying sizes, with tight fitting lids to eliminate the transfer of strong smells and flavours and prevent the surface of the ice cream from drying out. Use containers a little larger than the quantity of ice cream, to allow for beating during freezing and increased volume when frozen. A headspace of 2cm|¾in is adequate. Granita is the exception to this, as it requires as shallow a container as possible to reduce freezing time. Only use stainless steel or aluminium while making ice cream or sorbet as other metals can impart a metallic taste.

The freezer

An upright or chest domestic freezer is the essential item of equipment. For making ice cream the temperature should be -18°C|-66°F. A freezer thermometer is a very useful tool. The colder the freezer the more quickly the ice will freeze, making smaller ice crystals and smoother ice cream. If the freezer is badly packed the motor will have to work harder to maintain temperature.

Adding volume

1 Using a fork requires more effort, but is an effective way of increasing volume by introducing air into sorbet and granitas.

2 For making large quantities of ice cream, a hand-held electric whisk saves time and adds even more volume to the mixture.

For making parfait

You will need all the items for making ices, plus a good sugar thermometer; they can be expensive but do ensure perfect results. Choose one with a clip to hold it in place on the pan.

For making moulded iced desserts

Specialist equipment is available, but you can usually improvise with bowls and basins from your kitchen.

ICE CREAM MAKERS

These labour-saving electric machines vary greatly in price. The two basic types are those with a built-in freezing unit and those with a detachable double-skinned bowl which has to be pre-frozen before use. There are also ice cream machines that can be run inside a standard freezer. These have very poor motors and similar, if not better, results can be obtained by making ice cream by hand.

The most efficient – and most expensive – models are those with an integral freezing unit. Motors vary, depending on the make of the machine. If you are investing in an ice cream maker, choose the one with the most powerful motor and if possible see it in operation, as

noise levels vary considerably. As this type of ice cream maker tends to be larger than a food processor, working and storage space are prime considerations. These machines come with two bowls, a stainless-steel bowl built into the unit and a separate aluminium bucket that can be slotted into the larger fixed bowl. Most machines of this type have a see-through lid for easy viewing, plus a vent for pouring in additional ingredients. This plastic top simply slides off for easy washing.

RIGHT: *Ice cream maker with integral motor and freezing unit.*

Pre-freezing ice cream maker

For a slightly cheaper option, look out for a model with a detachable double-skinned bowl filled with freezing liquid. This type of machine will need to be frozen for at least 18 hours before use. When you are ready to use the ice cream maker, you simply fit the motor and paddle to the frozen bowl, switch on the power, and fill the bowl with the ice cream or sorbet mixture. It usually takes 25–40 minutes for the ice cream to churn.

If the freezer is large enough, the bowl can be stored there, giving the option to make home-made ice cream at any time. For larger quantities, it is very useful to have a second detachable bowl on standby and make two batches of ice cream.

When possible, eat the ice cream soon after it is made to fully enjoy the wonderful texture of machine-made ice cream.

ABOVE: *Simple ice cream maker with motorized paddles.*

FOR THE BEST RESULTS

- Pre-cool the machine or double-skinned bowl following the instructions given in the manufacturer's handbook.

- Chill all ice cream or water ice mixtures thoroughly before freezing; never add them to the machine while still warm.

- Do not overfill the ice cream maker.

- Allow plenty of room for ventilation while the machine is running.

Useful extras

Scoops

There are plenty of ice cream scoops on the market. Choose from half-moon-shaped stainless-steel scoops with sleek steel handles, simple spoon-shaped scoops with metal handles, easy-grip moulded plastic handles or brightly coloured plastic scoops with quick release levers. To be really impressive use silver scoops.

ABOVE: *Ice cream scoops are available in many different shapes, materials and colours.*

Cone moulds

For a really professional finish use wooden moulds. These are available only by mail order but you can improvise by making your own cone moulds from foil-covered cardboard.

ABOVE: *This wooden cone mould is a very simple but useful tool for making professional-looking cones.*

Melon ballers

Ice cream looks very attractive when scooped with a melon baller. Available from good cookshops in varying sizes, from pea to grape size, the larger size is best for ice cream. To make a ball, press the upturned cup into slightly softened ice cream, then rotate it. Arrange in a glass dish or on a plate, with fresh fruits.

ABOVE: *Use melon ballers to make miniature scoops of ice cream and sorbet, and pile them up on a plate.*

Kulfi moulds

Freeze Indian-style ice creams in these traditional kulfi moulds available from some large Indian supermarkets. You can also use lolly moulds, dariole moulds or plastic cups.

ABOVE: *Unmoulding kulfi is easy with a specially designed all-in-one kulfi mould.*

Basic Ingredients

Nothing beats the cool, creamy smoothness of the ultimate indulgence, home-made ice cream. The choice of flavours and flavour combinations is limited only by your own imagination, so begin with our basic formulae and adapt or develop them to incorporate all the tastes you love. You will rapidly build a repertoire of wonderful iced desserts, all completely additive-free and made with only the ingredients that you choose to be there.

Ice cream

Cream

You just couldn't make true ice cream without lashings of cream. Surprisingly, whipping cream, with its natural creamy taste, makes the best ice cream, especially when mixed with strong rich flavours such as coffee, toffee or chocolate. Double cream is, however, a must for vanilla or brown bread ice cream. Clotted cream and crème fraîche, the thick, rich lightly soured French-style cream, make delicious additions to fruit, honey and spice ice creams. Do be careful when using double or clotted cream as their high butter-fat content can give the ice cream a buttery flavour and texture, especially if it is overchurned. Avoid UHT creams as the flavour is so obvious and strong.

Milk

There is a wide choice of milks in most supermarkets, from skimmed, semi-skimmed, full-fat and breakfast milk to the now more readily available goat's milk and soya milk. Skimmed milk is best avoided when making ice cream at home, due to its low fat content and "thin" taste, but it is difficult to distinguish between semi-skimmed or full-fat milk, especially when they are mixed with cream. Full fat, semi-skimmed and goat's milk all make delicious ice cream.

Yogurt

The choice of yogurt is highly personal: it seems people either love ice cream which contains yogurt, or absolutely hate it! If you are not sure how your family will react, start with the mild bio-style natural yogurt, with its creamy smoothness, and, if that is successful, work up to the stronger, sharper sheep's and goat's milk yogurts.

ABOVE: *New-laid eggs and double or whipping cream gives home-made ice cream its luxury flavour.*

Cheeses

Light, virtually fat-free fromage frais can be added to fruit or vanilla ice creams and is ideal for those who adore ice cream but have to watch their fat intake. Ricotta, an Italian whey cheese, has a white, creamy, soft texture. It is rather like a cross between cottage and cream cheese and can be used successfully in certain ice creams. For the richest results of all, try mascarpone, another Italian cheese. It has a deep-buttery yellow colour and a texture similar to that of cream cheese. For the best of both worlds, mix mascarpone with fromage frais for a rich tasting, fat reduced dessert.

Non-dairy products

Look out for soya milk, either unsweetened or sweetened, in longlife cartons, and canned coconut milk – both ideal for vegans or those on a milk-free diet. Coconut milk is also a great standby for a dinner party ice cream when mixed with lime or lemon.

Eggs

Where possible use new-laid, organic eggs for the best colour and flavour. They cost very little more than ordinary eggs but do make such a difference to the finished result of home-made ice cream.

Sweeteners

Caster sugar has been used in the majority of the recipes, as its fine crystals dissolve quickly in the custard, maintaining a smooth, silky texture. Granulated sugar is used for making praline, a delicious ingredient in some of the speciality ices. Light brown and dark brown muscovado sugar can also be used as a sweetener in some recipes, where the darker colour and stronger flavour is used to great effect. Honey and maple syrup also make delicious additions, either on their own or mixed with caster sugar. They are particularly good in ice cream flavoured with nuts.

Cornflour

Many purists will throw their hands up in horror at the idea of cornflour being used in the custard for an ice cream. They might well argue that it is far better to make the custard in a double boiler or a large heatproof bowl set over simmering water. It is certainly true that cornflour is not a standard ingredient in a classic custard, but it does help to stabilize the custard and reduces the risk of curdling. Custard which contains a little cornflour is easier to handle, so can be gently cooked in a heavy-based pan. It will thicken in 4–5 minutes as against 15 minutes or more in a double boiler, greatly reducing the cooking time.

COOK'S TIP *Put leftover egg whites in a small plastic box. Cover with a tight-fitting lid and label the box clearly. Freeze up to 6 months and thaw at room temperature for 4 hours. Use to make pavlovas, meringues and meringue-based ice creams.*

Water ices

Sugar syrup

A simple sugar syrup is made by heating a mixture of caster sugar and water in a medium saucepan, stirring until the sugar has dissolved. It is no longer thought essential to boil the syrup, just to heat it for long enough to dissolve the sugar. Caster sugar has been used for syrups in the recipe section of this book because it dissolves very rapidly, but granulated sugar can also be used, as can light brown sugar or honey. Once made and cooled, the syrup can be stored in the fridge for several days.

Flavouring

Choose from a wide range of fresh fruit purées such as strawberry, raspberry, peach or pineapple, or mix with some of the more exotic fruits such as passion fruit, mango and lime. Dried fruits are sometimes steeped in apple or grape juice or in water and brandy or a liqueur mixture before being puréed. Citrus rinds (orange, lemon or lime) can be infused in the hot syrup for extra flavour and then fresh juice added to heighten and strengthen the flavour. Spice infusions or mixtures of spices and fruits also work very well and create unusual ices that are particularly successful with those that prefer a light dessert that is not too sweet.

ABOVE: *Honey can be used on its own or with sugar.*

Egg white

The purpose of adding egg white to a semi-frozen sorbet is twofold. Firstly, it helps to stabilize the mixture, which is important for those sorbets that melt quickly, and secondly, it can be used to lighten very dense or fibrous sorbets such as those made from blackcurrants or blackberries. The egg white requires only the minimum beating with a fork to loosen it and need not be beaten until frothy or standing in peaks as used to be suggested.

HOW TO SEPARATE AN EGG

Crack the egg on the side of a bowl. Gently ease the halves apart, keeping the yolk in one half and letting the white fall into the bowl below. Separate any remaining egg white from the yolk by swapping the yolk from one shell half to the other. Do this several times if necessary, until all the egg white has fallen into the bowl and what remains is the pure egg yolk. If you do drop any egg yolk into the bowl below, scoop it out with one of the eggshell halves; the jagged edges will trap the yolk and prevent it from sliding back into the bowl.

Preparing Ice Cream

Many classic ice creams are based on a custard made from eggs and milk. It is not difficult to make, but as it is used so frequently, it is worth perfecting by following these very simple guidelines.

How to make a classic ice cream

Making the custard-base

INGREDIENTS

FLAVOURING to INFUSE (optional)

300ml | ½ pint | 1¼ cups
SEMI-SKIMMED MILK

4 medium EGG YOLKS

75g | 3oz | 6 tbsp CASTER SUGAR

5ml | 1 tsp CORNFLOUR

BATCH COOKING

If you are planning to make ice cream for a party, make double quantities of custard to save time. It is not advisable, however, to increase the quantities any more than this or it would be difficult to heat the custard evenly. It is quicker and easier to make up two double quantity batches in separate pans and a lot safer than running the risk of curdling one pan of custard made with a dozen eggs!

1 Prepare any flavourings. Split vanilla pods with a sharp knife; crack coffee beans with a mallet. Cinnamon sticks, whole cloves, fresh rosemary and lavender sprigs or bay leaves can be used as they are.

2 Pour the milk into a saucepan. Bring it to the boil, then remove the pan from the heat, add the chosen flavouring and leave to infuse for 30 minutes or until cool.

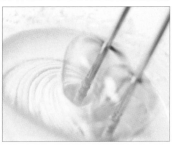

3 If you have used a vanilla pod, lift it out of the pan, and scrape the seeds back into the milk to enrich the flavour. Whisk the egg yolks, caster sugar and cornflour in a bowl until thick and foamy. Bring the plain or infused milk to the boil, then gradually whisk it into the yolk mixture. Pour the combined mixture back into the saucepan.

4 Cook the mixture over a low heat, stirring it continuously until it approaches boiling point and thickens to the point where the custard will coat the back of a wooden spoon. Do not let the custard overheat or it may curdle. Take the pan off the heat and continue stirring, making sure to take the spoon right around the bottom edges of the pan.

5 Pour the custard into a bowl and cover the surface with clear film to prevent the formation of a skin, or cover the surface with a light sprinkling of caster sugar. Leave to cool, then chill in the fridge until required. If you are making the ice cream in a machine, ensure the custard is chilled before starting.

COOK'S TIP *Reduce the temperature of custard by pouring it into a cool bowl. Stand this in a larger bowl of cold or iced water and change the water as it warms.*

RESCUING CURDLED CUSTARD

Quickly take the saucepan off the heat and plunge it into a sink or a roasting tin, half filled with cold water. Stir the custard frequently, taking the spoon right into the bottom edges of the pan. Keep stirring for 4–5 minutes until the temperature of the custard has dropped and the custard has stabilized. You may also find it helpful to whisk the mixture. If all else fails, sieve it.

Using flavourings

If you haven't infused the milk, you may wish to flavour the custard. To make chocolate custard, break white, dark or milk chocolate into pieces and stir these into the hot custard in the saucepan, off the heat. Stir occasionally for 5 minutes until the chocolate has melted completely, then pour the flavoured custard into a bowl, cover and cool. Chill in the fridge.

Other flavourings that can be added include strong coffee (either filter or instant dissolved in boiling water), flower waters such as orange flower water or rose water and sweeteners that also add flavour, such as maple syrup or honey. Vanilla, peppermint or almond essence are popular flavourings. These should be added to the custard after it has cooled.

FRUIT AND CREAM COMBINATIONS

Although you can make delicious fruit ice creams with a custard base, the combination of custard, cream and fruit purée can sometimes be too rich a combination and dull the fresh fruit flavour, robbing it of its intensity. Many cooks prefer to omit the custard and simply use sieved fresh berry fruit, simple purées or lightly poached and puréed orchard fruits stirred into whipped cream.

If you are making a fruit ice cream in an ice cream maker, you can speed up the churning time by partially freezing the purée before stirring in the cream.

Adding cream

If you are making ice cream in an ice cream maker, follow the preliminary instructions for your specific machine, pre-cooling the machine or chilling the bowl in the freezer. Stir whipping cream, whipped double cream or any soft cream cheeses into the chilled plain or flavoured custard and churn until firm.

Creams with a high fat proportion – double cream, clotted cream or crème fraîche – should only be added to ice creams that are partially frozen, as they have a tendency to become buttery if churned for too long. Double cream is sometimes added at the start, but only for small quantities and minimal churning times.

Make the ice cream by hand in a freezerproof container, by folding soft whipped cream into the chilled plain or flavoured custard and pouring the mixture into the tub. Allow enough space for beating the ice cream during freezing. Crème fraîche, clotted cream and cream cheeses can also be added at this stage.

Parfaits

Making a basic parfait

Made correctly, a parfait is a light, cream-based confection with a softer, smoother texture than ice cream. Unlike ice cream, it does not need beating during freezing, so is ideal for anyone who does not have an electric ice cream maker.

Parfaits are traditionally set in moulds, tall glasses, china dishes or, more recently, in edible chocolate cups. The secret of a good parfait lies in the sugar syrup. Dissolve the sugar gently without stirring so that it does not crystallize, then boil it rapidly until it registers 115°C | 239°F on a sugar thermometer, which is known as the soft ball stage.

Quickly whisk the syrup into the whisked eggs. Cook over hot water until very thick. Cool, then mix with flavourings, alcohol and whipped cream. Freeze until solid and serve straight from the freezer.

SERVES FOUR

INGREDIENTS

115g | 4oz | generous ½ cup CASTER SUGAR

120ml | 4fl oz | ½ cup WATER

4 medium EGG YOLKS

FLAVOURINGS

300ml | ½ pint | 1¼ cups DOUBLE CREAM

1 Mix the sugar and water in a saucepan. Heat gently, without stirring, until the sugar has dissolved completely. Meanwhile, half fill a medium saucepan with water and bring it to simmering point.

2 Bring the sugar syrup to the boil and boil it rapidly for 4–5 minutes until it starts to thicken. It will be ready to use when it registers 115°C | 239°F on a sugar thermometer, or will form a soft ball when dropped into water.

FLAVOURINGS

Traditionally flavoured with coffee or chocolate and a dash of brandy or whisky, parfaits are also delicious made with ground spices such as cinnamon with apple or ginger with banana. Double cream adds just the right degree of richness, although crème fraîche or whipping cream can also be used with very good results. Another traditional combination is fruit purées mixed with liqueurs such as kirsch, Cointreau or Grand Marnier; these make a sophisticated iced dessert at a dinner party.

3 Put the eggs in a heatproof bowl and whisk until frothy. Place over the simmering water and gradually whisk in the hot sugar syrup. Whisk steadily until creamy. Take off the heat and continue whisking until cool and the whisk leaves a trail across the surface when lifted.

4 Fold in the chosen flavourings, such as melted chocolate and brandy, ground cinnamon and coffee, whisky and chopped ginger, kirsch and raspberry purée or kir and strawberry purée. In a separate bowl, whip the cream lightly until it just holds its shape. Fold it into the mixture.

5 Pour the parfait mixture into moulds, dishes or chocolate-lined cases. Freeze for at least 4 hours or until firm. Decorate, if liked, with whipped cream, spoonfuls of crème fraîche, caramel shapes or chocolate-dipped fruits. Serve immediately.

COOK'S TIP *Double cream adds just the right degree of richness to parfaits, although crème fraîche or whipping cream can also be used with good results.*

Boiling sugar successfully

1 If you don't have a sugar thermometer, check whether the boiling sugar syrup has cooked to the right consistency, the soft ball stage, by lowering a spoon into it and then lifting it up. If the syrup falls steadily from the spoon it is not yet ready to use and if you were to add it to the eggs at this stage, the frozen parfait would set hard. Cook it for a little longer and check again with the spoon.

2 The syrup is ready to test for the soft ball stage when it looks tacky, and forms pliable strands when two spoons are dipped in it, back to back, and then pulled apart.

Take the pan off the heat and then test the boiling syrup by dropping a little of it into a bowl of iced water. The syrup should form a ball. Wait a few seconds until it cools, then lift the ball of solidified syrup out. You should be able to mould it with your fingertips.

3 Once the syrup has reached soft ball stage prevent it overcooking by plunging the base of the pan into cold water, either in a sink or in a shallow container. If the syrup is allowed to overcook it will crystallize in the pan and form brittle glass-like strands that snap. Adding over-cooked syrup to the eggs, will cause the mixture to solidify into a rock-solid mass that would be impossible to mix.

Freezing ice cream

Beating or churning

Freezing is obviously a crucial stage in the making of a home-made ice cream, and there are two basic methods. Freezing without a machine is also known as "still freezing", while the action in an ice cream maker is "stir freezing". We are so used to electrical machines that it is hard to envisage how labour-intensive it must have been for the cooks of one hundred or more years ago beating ice cream by hand in churns stood in packed ice hewn from frozen rivers. Making ice cream by hand today requires freezing it in a tub or similar container and beating it several times during the freezing process. It is this beating or churning process that is done automatically in an ice cream maker.

The secret of a really good ice cream is the formation of minute ice crystals. The finished ice cream should be light and taste cold, not icy. If the ice crystals are large, the ice cream will have a grainy, coarse texture, which will detract from the creamy, smooth taste you are aiming to achieve. Beating the ice cream, either by hand or with an ice cream maker, breaks down the crystals. The more it is beaten while it is freezing, the finer and silkier the finished texture will be.

Freezing with an ice cream maker

1 Having prepared your ice cream maker according to the manufacturer's instructions, pour the chilled custard and whipping cream into the bowl, fit the paddle, fix on the lid and begin churning.

2 After 10–15 minutes of churning, the ice cream will have begun to freeze. The mixture will thicken and will start to look slushy. Continue to churn the mixture in the same way.

3 After 20–25 minutes, the ice cream will be considerably thicker. It will still be too soft to scoop, but this is the ideal stage to mix in your chosen additional flavourings, such as praline or browned breadcrumbs.

Preparing Water Ices

Sorbets, like water ices, are made with a light sugar syrup flavoured with fruit juice, fruit purée, wine, liqueur, tea or herbs. They should not contain milk or cream, and are best made in an ice cream maker, as the constant churning ensures that the ice crystals are as tiny as possible.

Sorbet

Making a basic sorbet

SERVES SIX

INGREDIENTS

150–200g | 5–7oz | ¾–1cup CASTER SUGAR

200–300ml | 7–10fl oz | ¾–1¼ cups WATER

FLAVOURING

1 EGG WHITE

FRUIT PURÉES

As an approximate guide, 500g | 1¼lb | 5 cups of berry fruits will produce about 450ml | ¾ pint | scant 2 cups purée. Mix this with 115g–150g | 4–5oz | generous ½–¾ cup caster sugar (depending on the natural acidity of the fruit), which has been dissolved in 300ml | ½ pint | 1¼ cups boiling water and then made up to 1 litre | 1¾ pints | 4 cups with extra cold water, lemon or lime juice.

1 Put the sugar and water in a medium saucepan and heat the mixture, stirring, until the sugar has just dissolved.

2 Add pared citrus rinds, herbs or spices, depending on your chosen flavouring. Leave to infuse. Strain and cool, then chill well in the fridge. Mix with additional flavourings such as fruit juices, sieved puréed fruits, herbs or tea.

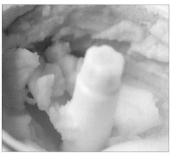

3 USING AN ICE CREAM MAKER: Pour the syrup mixture into the machine and churn until it is thick but still too soft to scoop.

4 USING AN ICE CREAM MAKER: Lightly beat the egg white with a fork and pour it into the ice cream maker, either adding it through the top vent or removing the lid and stirring it in, depending on the method recommended by the manufacturer of your machine. Continue churning the sorbet until it is firm enough to scoop with a spoon.

5 BY HAND: Pour the mixture into a plastic tub or similar freezerproof container. It should not be more than 4cm | 1½in deep. Cover and freeze in the coldest part of the freezer for 4 hours or until it has partially frozen and ice crystals have begun to form. Beat until smooth with a fork, or hand-held electric whisk. Alternatively, process in a food processor until smooth.

6 BY HAND: Lightly beat the egg white and stir it into the sorbet. Freeze for a further 4 hours or until firm enough to scoop.

COOK'S TIP *If making by hand, ensure that the freezer temperature is as low as possible to speed up the freezing process, and beat at regular intervals.*

Granitas

Making a citrus granita

This wonderfully refreshing, simple Italian-style water ice has the fine texture of snow and is most often served piled into pretty glass dishes. You don't need fancy or expensive equipment, just a medium saucepan, a sieve or blender for puréeing the fruit, a fork and room in the freezer for a large plastic container.

INGREDIENTS

There are no hard-and-fast rules when it comes to the proportions of sugar to water, nor is there a standard amount of flavouring which must be added. Unlike sorbets, granitas consist largely of water, with just enough sugar to sweeten them and prevent them from freezing too hard. A total of 1 litre | 1¾ pints | 4 cups of flavoured sugar syrup will provide six generous portions of granita.

1 Squeeze the juice from six lemons, oranges or four ruby grapefruit. Add 115–200g | 4–7oz | generous ½–1 cup caster sugar, the precise amount will depend on the natural acidity of the fruit. Dissolve the sugar in 300ml | ½ pint | 1¼ cups boiling water, then mix it with the citrus juice and rind. Top up to 1 litre | 1¾ pints | 4 cups with extra water or water and alcohol. Add enough alcohol to taste but don't be over generous or the granita will not freeze.

2 Pour the chilled mixture into a large plastic tub or similar freezerproof container. It should not be more than 2–2.5cm | ¾–1in deep. Freeze it in the coldest part of the freezer for 2 hours until it is mushy around the edges.

Take the container out of the freezer and beat the granita well with a fork to break up the ice crystals. Return the granita to the freezer. Beat it at 30 minute intervals for the next 2 hours until it has the texture of snow.

Making a hot infusion

Some of the most delicious granitas are based on hot mixtures. Coffee is just one example. Pour hot, strong filtered coffee into a bowl or saucepan and stir in sugar to taste. For a ginger granita, infuse finely chopped root ginger in boiling water, then sweeten it. Chocolate granita is made by mixing cocoa powder to a smooth paste with a little boiling water and sweetening to taste. All hot infusions must be left to cool, then chilled in the fridge before being frozen.

Making a fruit-flavoured granita

To make a fruit-flavoured granita, purée berry fruits such as raspberries or strawberries, then sieve the purée to remove the seeds. Alternatively, purée ripe peaches, then sieve to remove the skins. To make a melon granita, scoop the seeds out of orange- or green-fleshed melons, then purée the flesh. Peeled and seeded watermelon can be puréed in the same way, or the flesh can be puréed along with the seeds and then sieved afterwards.

SERVING AND STORING GRANITAS

Coffee granita is classically served in a tumbler with a spoonful of whipped cream on top. Other types of granita look pretty spooned into tall glasses and decorated with fresh fruits or herb leaves and flowers. Because of its soft, snow-like texture, a granita is best served as soon as it is made. If this is not possible, you can leave it for a couple of hours in the freezer, beating it once or twice more if convenient. If you must freeze a granita overnight or for even longer, let it thaw slightly and beat it really well with a fork before serving. The ice crystals will become smaller but the taste will be the same. As a granita does not contain dairy products there are fewer concerns with food contamination or deterioration.

COOK'S TIP *Before you make the granita, make sure that the container you choose will fit in your freezer. A new stainless steel roasting tin can be used to freeze the granita mixture. As this metal is such a good conductor the granita will freeze very much faster than it would in a plastic container. Do not use aluminium as the metal could react with the fruit acids to give a metallic taste to the finished granita.*

Serving Ice Creams and Sorbets

Impress your friends at your next supper or dinner party by trying one of the following serving suggestions. They are not difficult to achieve, but look stunningly professional.

Oval shapes

These quenelle shapes are very easy to make and look attractive especially when three different flavours of ice cream or sorbet are used. Arrange them on a plate flooded with chocolate sauce or Melba sauce and complete the picture with a sprig of redcurrants, a few whole fruits, a mint leaf or a few pieces of chocolate caraque.

1 You need two deep dessertspoons. Take a scoop of ice cream with one spoon. Slide the second spoon underneath the ice cream, transferring the oval, then repeat the process.

2 Gently ease the ice cream oval on to a plate, then draw the edge of the spoon along the top of the ice cream to create a decorative line.

Shavings

Pare off long shavings of ice cream or sorbet by pressing a dessertspoon into the surface and dragging it at an angle of 45°. Mixtures that are soft-set, can be scooped straight from the freezer, but in most cases ice cream or sorbet should be allowed to soften slightly before being scooped.

Using a melon baller

1 Press a medium or large melon baller into the frozen sorbet, rotate it, then put the ball in a dessert glass or serving dish.

2 Add more balls in the same way, piling them up attractively. Decorate with wafer biscuits or mint leaves dusted with icing sugar.

3 Another very effective presentation is to arrange balls of grape juice or apple sorbet on a flat plate to look like a bunch of grapes, adding a grape, strawberry or mint leaf to the top.

4 Balls of raspberry sorbet arranged in a circle on a plate flooded with apricot sauce look wonderful, especially when the centre is filled with fresh raspberries.

Using an ice cream scoop

Dip the scoop into warm water, press it into the ice cream and run the scoop along the surface, pressing it against the side of the ice cream container until a well rounded scoop has been formed. Put this on a serving dish. Rinse the ice cream scoop and continue.

Piping shapes

Whirls of sorbet can be piped straight on to serving plates or into fruit cases or chocolate moulds from a large piping bag fitted with a cream nozzle. The ice cream or sorbet must be soft enough to pipe, so choose a variety that will not melt too quickly. If you are using sorbet, you may need to set it slightly with a little gelatine before piping and freezing it.

Creating a bed of ice

On very hot summer days, keep ice cream and sorbets cold by scooping them into dishes set over a plate or shallow dish filled with crushed ice. To crush the ice, wrap ice cubes in a clean dish towel and break them up by hitting them with a rolling pin. Keep the chunks of ice fairly large so that they will not melt too quickly.

Using citrus shells

1 Colourful fruit shells look very pretty filled with sorbet. Cut the top off a lemon, lime or orange, loosen the edges of the flesh with a small, sharp knife then scoop out all the flesh with a teaspoon, taking care to keep the shell intact. Having prepared more shells in the same way, rinse them all with cold water and drain them well. Use the flesh in another dessert.

2 Pipe or spoon the prepared sorbet into the hollowed fruit shells, wrap them in clear film and freeze them until they are needed. Serve each sorbet garnished with a tiny sprig of fresh mint. Freeze with the "lids" replaced, if you like.

3 If you have a cannelle knife, you can cut decorative grooves in the skin of the fruit before cutting a slice off the top, hollowing out the centres and filling them with sorbet.

COOK'S TIP *Do not be tempted to repeatedly thaw ice cream until it is soft enough to scoop and then refreeze the leftovers. The rich dairy content and fluctuating temperature will make this the perfect breeding ground for bacteria.*

SERVING TEMPERATURE

We have all been faced at some time with a tub of ice cream that is just too hard to serve. The majority of home-made ice creams will freeze very hard, so it is worth taking the ice cream out of the freezer and transferring it to the fridge for 20 minutes or so before serving, or while you eat your main course. This allows the ice cream to soften slightly and also to "ripen", so that the full flavour of the ice cream can be enjoyed. Alternatively, it can be thawed slightly in a microwave for 2–3 minutes on the defrost setting or for 1 minute on full power and then left at room temperature for 10 minutes. If you forget, serve the ice cream by dipping the scoop into a jug of hot water each time you form a ball of ice cream.

Flavourings for Ices

Visit a modern ice cream parlour and you'll be dazzled by the number of flavours available. Yet this has no comparison to the endless possibilities you can create at home. Spices, herbs, fruits of every kind, flower waters, chocolate, coffee and nuts can all be used – singly or in combination. Experiment to find the tastes you and your family like best, remembering that freezing dulls some flavours, so you can often afford to be bold.

Herbs and flowers

Edible flowers

A sprinkling of just a few petals or tiny flower heads from the garden can turn even a few simple scoops of home-made strawberry or vanilla ice cream into a dinner party dessert. A few vibrant pansies or tiny violas mixed with primrose petals or even a few dainty violets would be perfect for a springtime party, while pastel-coloured rose petals, borage flowers or sprigs of lavender would make a fine decoration in summer, as would a misty haze of elderflowers or sweet cicely flowers. For something bolder, use yellow or orange marigold petals (but not French marigolds) or nasturtiums. If selecting other flowers, please be aware that not all flowers are edible. Avoid plants which grow from a bulb or which would not be found in a herb garden.

Flower waters

Orange flower or orange blossom water and rose water add a delicate fragrance to ground almond or summer berry ice creams and sorbets. Add a few drops and seal the bottle well to prevent evaporation.

Herbs

Rosemary, bay, mint and lavender make wonderful additions to creamy ice creams, sherbets or sorbets. For best results infuse a few sprigs of rosemary or lavender, two to three whole bay leaves or a small bunch of fresh mint in cream or sugar syrup which has just come to the boil. Leave in the liquid until cool, then sieve. You can also add a little fresh chopped mint or other extra herbs to the finished ice cream or sorbet.

RIGHT: *Sprigs of flowers or flower water give a delicate flavour to ice creams and sorbets.*

Spices

Ginger

TYPES/FORMS: The rhizome of an elegant tropical plant, ginger appears in many guises. The root is widely available fresh and is also preserved in sugar syrup as stem ginger. Chopped candied ginger and crystallized ginger are other forms of this delicious spice.

USES: Ginger makes a wonderful ice cream ingredient just on its own but it gives a glorious lift to fruit ices, especially with fruit such as rhubarb or pears and it is a natural partner for tropical fruit. Preserved ginger, ginger syrup and ginger wine make delicious ice cream sauces.

PREPARATION: Peel root ginger, then slice or chop it thinly. Alternatively, grate it with the fine-tooth surface of a grater. Slice or chop preserved stem ginger; finely chop candied or crystallized ginger if pieces are large.

Using ginger

1 Peel away the skin on the ginger root, using a swivel-blade vegetable peeler or a small, sharp knife. Take care when peeling to remove only the thin outer skin.

2 Grate the ginger on the fine section of a regular grater or a nutmeg grater. This is easiest to do if the ginger is frozen. It will thaw instantly on being grated.

Vanilla

TYPES/FORMS: Seed pods of the climbing vanilla orchid plant are sold singly or in pairs. The spice is also finely ground, mixed with sugar and sold in sachets labelled vanilla sugar. It is best known, however, as vanilla essence.

The pods are picked while still unripe. On drying, their yellow colour deepens to a dark brown and they acquire a natural coating of vanillin crystals, which are the source of the characteristic spicy aroma. The word "vanilla" comes from the Spanish "*vainilla*", meaning "little sheath". Although always associated with sweet dishes, the vanilla pod is not itself sweet.

Beware of cheap vanilla flavourings as their harsh, almost bitter, flavour can be overpowering and could spoil the delicate flavour of some ice creams. The better quality vanilla essence is always labelled "natural vanilla essence".

USES: Vanilla is delicious in ice cream, whipped cream and custard and is used extensively when making patissiere cream and confectionery.

PREPARATION: Slit the whole vanilla pod, add it to cream or milk that has just come to the boil, then leave to cool and infuse. Lift up the pod, and holding it over the liquid, scrape the tiny black seeds with a small knife so that they fall into the liquid. The flavoured cream or milk makes excellent ice cream. Don't throw pods away after use. Rinse under cold water, pat dry with kitchen paper and store two or three in a jar of caster sugar to make your own vanilla sugar. Vanilla essence is highly concentrated and you only need 2.5–5ml | ½–1 tsp for ice cream.

Cinnamon

TYPES/FORMS: Cinnamon is obtained from the bark of the cinnamon tree, which is native to India. The bark is rolled into sticks or quills and dried. Cinnamon is also sold finely ground. The ground spice is seldom used in ice creams, except as a decoration, although it is widely used in baking. Cassia is a related spice. It resembles cinnamon in terms of aroma and flavour but is coarser and more pungent. Cassia is usually cheaper than cinnamon.

USES: Ice cream may not be the obvious use for cinnamon, a spice better known as an ingredient in cakes, biscuits and savoury dishes, but it adds a delicious flavour, especially with fruits such as peaches or nectarines.

PREPARATION: Infuse halved cinnamon sticks in milk or cream that has just come to the boil. When it has imparted its flavour, strain the milk or cream and use it to make custard as the basis for ice cream. Cinnamon sticks can also be used to flavour fruit purées or compotes by infusing in the liquid in the same way.

Using vanilla

Using a sharp knife, slit a whole vanilla pod. Add it to milk or cream that has just come to the boil. For maximum flavour, scrape out the tiny black seeds from the pod and let them fall into the milk or cream.

Nutmeg

TYPES/FORMS: Sold whole, nutmegs are the dried seeds of the fruit of the nutmeg tree, which is native to the tropics. Blades of mace, the pretty orange outer coating, are also sold separately, and both are sold ground.

USES: Nutmeg's wonderfully aromatic and slightly bitter flavour complements both sweet and savoury dishes. It is delicious in milk-based desserts such as ice cream.

PREPARATION: For the best flavour, grate a little off a whole nutmeg as and when you need it, using a fine-toothed surface of a grater or, better still, a small nutmeg grater. Ready ground nutmeg rapidly loses its pungency when stored.

Star anise

These pretty star-shaped pods are a favourite of Chinese cooks, but are becoming popular in the West. Use them whole for sauces and compotes or infuse them in sugar syrups or custards for ices with a lovely aniseed flavour.

Using cardamom

Traditionally used in Indian, Arabian and North African cooking, cardamom also adds a wonderful delicate aromatic fragrance to sorbets, ice creams and fruit compotes. If the recipe calls for cardamom seeds, crush the pods with the back of a cook's knife until they split. If necessary, use the tip of the knife to remove any remaining seeds from the pods. Use both the pod and the seeds for maximum flavour.

Cloves

TYPES/FORMS: The unopened flower buds of a tree related to the myrtle, cloves look like tiny nails. They are available whole and ground.

USES: Although cloves are most commonly used in savoury dishes, they are also widely used in desserts, particularly with apples and other fruits. Their pungent flavour means that they are a somewhat unlikely ingredient in ice cream, but if used sparingly, they add an intriguing flavour.

PREPARATION: Infuse whole cloves in milk or cream. This is especially appropriate when making a custard to form the basis of a fruit ice cream. Don't overdo this flavouring – the taste should be subtle and not strident.

Lemon grass

Mainly known for the delicate lemon fragrance it contributes to Thai and Vietnamese cookery, lemon grass is now widely available. Most supermarkets stock the fresh stems, which are pale green and tipped with white; it is also available as dried whole stems or ground lemon grass and sold in jars. To extract the delicate flavour the dried stems must be soaked in warm water for at least two hours before use. Fresh lemon grass can be finely sliced or crushed and infused in the milk to be used for custard-based ice creams or infused in the sugar syrup for a granita or sorbet.

Chocolate

CHOOSING THE BEST

A chocolate with a good, strong flavour is vital when making ice creams as the flavour of the chocolate is dulled when it is mixed with custard and cream. For the best and strongest flavour choose a good quality dark or bitter chocolate with a high proportion of cocoa solids. Confectioners and good food shops will have a selection of superior chocolates but many of the larger supermarkets now stock several different types of good quality cooking chocolate. Choose one with "luxury" or "Belgian" on the label as it will almost certainly have at least 75% cocoa solids and good flavour and taste will be guaranteed.

Chocolate Menier can also be used. It has a stronger flavour and is less sweet than some other types of chocolate, but is well suited to ice cream making. Plain dessert chocolate contains between 30 and 60% cocoa solids. Check the side of the pack for details – the higher the cocoa solids, the stronger the chocolate flavour will be, so avoid using any chocolate with less than 45% cocoa solids if possible.

In general, chocolate cake coverings should be avoided, as these have a mild, less chocolatey taste. With their added vegetable fat, they are more suited to making chocolate curls or caraque. What you can do, however, is to mix cake covering with an equal quantity of luxury dark chocolate. This way, you get the easy melting and moulding qualities of the former, coupled with the superior taste of the latter.

How to melt chocolate

Couverture

This pure chocolate contains no fats other than cocoa butter. It is used mainly by professionals and is only available from specialist suppliers. It generally requires "tempering" before use to distribute the cocoa fat evenly. This is quite a lengthy process that involves warming and working the chocolate until it reaches 32°C | 90°F. Couverture is usually used for moulding or decorating because of its glossy finish. It is available as white, milk and dark chocolate drops or as a block.

White chocolate

As when buying dark chocolate, choose "luxury" white chocolate or "Swiss" white chocolate for the best flavour. White chocolate is made from cocoa butter extracted during the production of cocoa solids. Although it includes about 2% cocoa solids many purists would argue that this is not nearly enough to make it a true chocolate, especially as the cocoa butter is then mixed with milk solids, sugar and flavourings.

As a result of these additional ingredients, white chocolate does require extra care when being melted: it quickly hardens if overheated. Do check the pack before buying, and choose a brand with a minimum of 25% cocoa butter, as any chocolate with less than this will be difficult to melt. The more cocoa butter there is the creamier and softer the chocolate will be. Some brands may even include vegetable fat or oils, so always check the ingredients list.

Melting chocolate in a microwave

Break dark or milk chocolate into squares, and place them in a bowl that can be safely used in a microwave. Heat it on Full Power allowing 2 minutes for 115g | 4oz chocolate; 3 minutes for 200g | 7oz. The chocolate will retain its shape until you stir it. Don't be tempted to heat if for longer or you may spoil the chocolate. White chocolate melts easily and is best microwaved on Medium Power or in a bowl placed over a saucepan of "just boiled" water.

1 Pour water into a saucepan until it is about one third full. Bring to the boil, turn the heat off, then fit a heatproof bowl over the pan, making sure that the water does not touch the base of the bowl. Break the chocolate into pieces and put it in the bowl.

2 Leave the chocolate pieces for 4–5 minutes, without stirring, until the chocolate has melted, the chocolate pieces will hold their shape. Stir the chocolate briefly before folding it into ice cream, or using it as the basis of a sauce.

Cocoa

This rich, strong, dark powder is made by extracting some of the cocoa butter during chocolate production. What remains is a block containing around 20% cocoa butter, but this varies with each manufacturer. The cocoa is then ground and mixed with sugar and starch. The addition of starch means that cocoa needs to be cooked briefly to remove the raw, floury taste. This can be done by mixing it to a paste with a little boiling water, which is the usual technique when flavouring ice cream. If the cocoa is to be used in a sauce, it will probably be mixed with hot milk.

The very best cocoa is produced in Holland. It is alkalized, a process that removes the acidity and produces a cocoa with a mellow, well-rounded flavour. The technique was devised by the manufacturer, Van Houten, some 150 years ago and this is still the very best cocoa available. Although it is more expensive than some other brands, it is definitely worth using for ice cream and chocolate sauces.

Milk chocolate

Mild and creamy, milk chocolate is made with up to 40% milk or milk products and contains less cocoa solids than dark chocolate. Because it has a mild flavour, you will need to add more than when using dark chocolate. You can use a combination of melted milk chocolate and chopped milk chocolate. As with white chocolate, the addition of milk products means that it requires more careful heating than dark chocolate.

Carob

Although not a true chocolate, carob is viewed by many as an acceptable alternative. It is the ground seedpod of the carob or locust tree and can be used as a chocolate substitute. Usually available from health food shops and sold in bars or in a powdered form as a flour. If you are using a bar, be cautious as it is highly concentrated. The flour can be used in a similar way to cocoa.

STORING CHOCOLATE

Wrap opened packs of chocolate well or pack them in a plastic box. Store in a cool, dry place away from foods with very strong flavours, such as spices, which may taint the chocolate. Avoid very cold places or the chocolate may develop a dull whitish bloom. Chocolate has a long shelf life, but check use-by dates before cooking.

Fruits

Soft berry fruits

TYPES/FORMS: Berry fruits make marvellous ice creams and sorbets. You can choose from standard raspberries, larger tayberries and loganberries, bright red strawberries and tiny alpine and Hautbois strawberries, blueberries and blackberries. Look out for golden raspberries, too. These tend to be grown in small quantities by keen gardeners and are often difficult to find in the shops, but they are well worth trying when available.

USES: Delicious in ice creams, sorbets and sherbets, berry fruits can easily be transformed into superb sauces. Melba sauce is an obvious example, but there are plenty more to choose from. A delectable iced summer pudding that teams sliced strawberries with strawberry ice cream and soft fruit sorbet makes perfect use of summer fruits. Blueberries and red berries look most attractive sprinkled over ice cream sundaes or crushed and added to just setting ice cream for added texture and colour. Expensive alpine and Hautbois strawberries can be used for decoration only.

PREPARATION: Purée ripe fruits, press them through a fine sieve to remove the seeds, then use the purée in ice creams, sherbets or sorbets. Berry fruit purées are also delicious spooned over ice cream or mixed with a sugar syrup and lemon juice for a refreshing ice cream sauce.

RIGHT: *Redcurrants.*

MAKING A FRUIT PURÉE

Purée berry fruits in a food processor or blender until smooth, then press the purée through a sieve into a large bowl, using the back of a large spoon or ladle.

Cane fruits

TYPES/FORMS: This category includes black, red and white currants, green gooseberries and the more unusual red gooseberries. As their short midsummer season is soon over, enjoy them while they are available fresh and bursting with rich flavour.

USES: All cane fruits make good ice creams, sherbets and sorbets. They can also be used to make coulis and sauces. Currants look beautiful and are often used for decoration.

PREPARATION: Gently remove currants from their stems, using the tines of a fork. As blackcurrants have such a sharp flavour, it is wise to poach them first with sugar and a little water until just tender. Red and white currants can be eaten raw or lightly poached. Gooseberries should be topped and tailed with scissors before being cooked. Purée and sieve currants or cooked gooseberries if adding to ice cream, sorbet or sherbet. Gooseberry ice cream made with clotted cream is a wonderful summertime treat.

Orchard fruits

TYPES/FORMS: Choose from apples, pears, plums, damsons, cherries, apricots, peaches and nectarines.

USES: Orchard fruits, particularly peaches and nectarines, make irresistible ices. Use them in creamy ice creams, sorbets and similar desserts, with a little liqueur, if you like.

PREPARATION: Apples and pears should be peeled and cored; plums, peaches and apricots should be halved and stoned. The fruit should then be poached in a little water and sugar until tender before being processed to a smooth purée. Ripe peaches, nectarines and apricots can be puréed raw, then sieved to remove the skins. Damsons are small and fiddly to prepare, so poach, then scoop out the stones. Alternatively, press the cooked fruit through a sieve to remove the stones. Use stoned cherries whole or roughly chopped. Larger fruits can be used for decoration, provided they are ripe. Slice or chop them if necessary, and toss apples and pears in a little lemon juice to prevent discoloration.

How to stone and string cherries

1 Remove cherry stones easily with this handy gadget which pushes the stones out of the fruit. Usually available from good cookshops.

2 Cherries threaded on a skewer or cocktail stick make an attractive decoration, especially for an iced drink.

Citrus fruits

TYPES/FORMS: Choose from lemons, limes, oranges, tangerines, clementines, kumquats and grapefruit.

USES: All citrus fruit can be used to make sorbets, granitas and sherbets. In addition, oranges make a very good ice cream. Citrus fruit can also be used to make sauces, and the rind is frequently used as a decoration.

PREPARATION: Grate the rind or pare it thinly, taking care to remove only the coloured skin, leaving the bitter white pith behind. Cut the fruit in half and squeeze it, then strain the juice to remove any pips. Mix it with cream and custard for ice cream or with sugar syrup for sorbets, sherbets and granitas. Kumquats can be poached whole or in slices and used to accompany iced desserts.

RIGHT: *The juice and rind of lemons and limes add a refreshingly tart flavour to sorbets and ice creams.*

Rhubarb

TYPES/FORMS: Strictly speaking, these pretty pink stems are not a fruit at all but a vegetable. For making iced desserts, choose the early forced rhubarb with its delicate flavour and baby-pink stems. Maincrop rhubarb has thicker, darker stems and a coarser texture.

USES: Puréed cooked rhubarb makes an excellent sorbet and granita, or flavour it with ginger for an old-fashioned ice cream. Lightly poached rhubarb can be served as an accompaniment to vanilla, cinnamon or goat's milk ice cream.

PREPARATION: Both early forced and maincrop rhubarb need to be cooked with sugar and just a tablespoon or two of water.

Melons

TYPES/FORMS: Choose from Canteloupe, Charantais, Galia and Ogen melons. Test them for ripeness by pressing the stalk area of the skin. The melon should smell quite perfumed.

USES: With their delicate perfume, melons make the most wonderfully refreshing sorbets and granitas. The shells make excellent and attractive containers for serving melon ices.

PREPARATION: Cut them in half, scoop out the seeds, then purée the flesh before use. Watermelons can also be used, but as the seeds are speckled throughout the flesh it is often easier to leave them in when processing the fruit. Sieving the purée will remove them. As watermelons have rather a bland flavour, mix the purée with grated lime rind and juice.

How to segment an orange or grapefruit

1 Using a sharp knife, start by cutting a slice off the top and bottom of the orange or grapefruit.

2 Using a small serrated knife, slice off the skin and pith cleanly. Work your way from the top down to the base of the fruit.

3 Holding the fruit over a bowl to catch the juices, carefully cut between the membranes to remove the whole fruit segments.

Tropical fruits

TYPES/FORMS: Choose from bananas, pineapples, mangoes, passion fruit, grapes and kiwi fruit. These fruits are available year-round and are a welcome alternative to seasonal fruits.

USES: Mash peeled bananas or purée them with a little lemon or lime rind to prevent discoloration and make them into smooth ice creams with honey, ginger, chocolate or cinnamon. Puréed or chopped pineapple flesh makes wonderful ice cream, especially when chunky pieces of crushed meringue or a few tablespoons of rum are added. Pineapple can also be puréed and made into sorbets. Look out for the extra sweet varieties, with their bright yellow flesh. Mix puréed mango with ginger, lime or coconut for a sorbet with a Caribbean flavour. Grapes and kiwi fruit are best served as a colourful accompaniment to iced desserts, although both can be made into sorbet.

PREPARATION: Sliced or diced tropical fruits can be used as a decoration or sautéed in a little butter and sugar and then flamed in a little brandy, rum or orange liqueur for an easy ice cream accompaniment.

PREPARING PASSION FRUITS AND PINEAPPLES

Passion fruits are easy to prepare. Just slice them in half and scoop out the fragrant seeds with a teaspoon. If necessary, press the pulp through a sieve.

To prepare pineapples, slice the top off the pineapple, then cut it into slices of the desired width. Cut away the rind with a small sharp knife. Cut away any remaining eyes from the edges of the pineapple slices.

Remove the central core of each slice with an apple corer, pastry cutter or knife.

Preparing a mango

1 Place the mango, narrow side down, on a board. Cut a thick, lengthways slice off the sides, keeping the knife blade as close to the central stone as possible. Turn the mango round and repeat on the other side.

2 Make criss-cross cuts in the mango flesh, cutting down only as far as the skin, then turn the large slices of mango inside out so that the diced flesh stands proud. Scoop it into a bowl.

3 Cut all the remaining fruit away from the stone, remove the skin and dice the flesh.

Dried fruits

TYPES/FORMS: Sultanas, raisins, prunes, apricots, peaches, dates and figs are all suitable, as are dried apples and pears, although these are seldom used for making ice creams and sorbets. Several types of dried fruit are sold in vacuum packs labelled "ready to eat" and these do not need soaking before use, although they are sometimes macerated in wine or liqueur for extra flavour. More unusual dried fruit includes mango, cranberries and blueberries.

USES: Using dried fruits in ice creams is nothing new – rum and raisin is a classic combination. Drying fruits such as peaches and apricots intensifies their flavour, so they make excellent purées. These can either be incorporated in ice creams or sorbets, or used as sauces for any ice cream dessert.

PREPARATION: Use the smaller varieties of dried fruit whole or chopped, and steep them in fruit juice, wine, spirits or liqueur if you like. Larger fruits such as apricots and peaches need to be soaked and puréed before being added to ice cream, although chopped fruit can be added when the ice cream is partially frozen to give extra texture and colour.

Glacé fruits and candied peel

These vibrant, jewel-like fruits make a pretty addition to partially frozen ice cream, and are the traditional flavouring in the classic Italian Tutti Frutti Ice Cream. They can also be used to decorate elaborate ice cream sundaes. Most fruits can be glacéd and a wide selection is available in supermarkets and cookshops. Choose from glacé cherries of various colours, glacé or candied pineapple and candied fruit peels. Large whole or sliced glacé fruits tend to be expensive, but are great for special occasion desserts. Sugar is a natural preservative and glacé fruits will keep well in an airtight container, but they are best used as soon as possible and purchased fresh as needed.

Using glacé fruits

Use a small, sharp knife to finely chop the glacé fruits, then fold on to just setting vanilla ice cream for a classic Tutti Frutti.

Nuts

Nuts

TYPES/FORMS: Choose from a wide range of whole nuts such as almonds, hazelnuts, pistachios, walnuts and pecans, plus the less widely used macadamias, Brazil nuts and unsalted peanuts.

USES: Nuts are most popular in cream-based ice creams and are seldom added to water ices. Add chunky toasted nuts or praline for extra crunch in ice creams, or sprinkle them over elaborate ice cream sundaes. Roughly chopped sugared almonds with pastel-coloured coatings look good and make an easy decoration. Ground nuts infused in milk or cream give a delicate flavour to ice creams that are inspired by recipes from the Middle East.

PREPARATION: Toast the nuts, chop them roughly and fold them into partially frozen ice cream. Alternatively, use them to make praline, which can be broken up and folded into ice cream that is on the verge of setting. Finely ground almonds or cashews can be added to just boiled milk or cream, then left to cool. The flavoured milk can be strained or used as is to make a custard-based ice cream.

BELOW: Pistachio nuts are an attractive addition to ice cream.

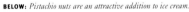

Blanched nuts

1 Put nuts such as pistachios or almonds into a bowl and pour over just enough boiling water to cover. Leave to stand for a minute or two until the skins expand and soften.

COOK'S TIP *Canned coconut milk combines convenience and full flavour for an ice cream that tastes good and is very easy to make.*

2 Drain the nuts. To pop nuts such as almonds out of their skins, simply pinch them. Skin pistachios by tipping them into a dish towel and rubbing them together.

Toasted nuts

For maximum flavour, toast whole or roughly chopped nuts in a dry frying pan on the hob, in a shallow cake tin under the grill or on a baking sheet in a medium oven until golden and lightly roasted. There is no need to add oil, as they have such a high natural oil content. Desiccated coconut can also be toasted in this way but because it is so finely processed you will need to keep a very close eye on it. It browns in a matter of seconds.

Spread out whole, sliced or roughly chopped nuts on a baking tin or sheet. Grill for 3–4 minutes, shaking the tin or sheet frequently so that the nuts brown evenly.

Making praline

1 Put granulated sugar, whole nuts and a little water into a heavy-based frying pan. Heat gently, without stirring. Do not use caster sugar and do not stir as this would cause the sugar to crystallize, making it solidify and become opaque. Continue to heat the sugar, but don't be tempted to stir the mixture with a spoon. Tilt the pan gently if necessary, to mix any sugar that has not dissolved completely.

2 Keep a watchful eye over the nuts as the sugar and nuts begin to turn golden. Remember to keep the heat low.

3 Quickly pour the praline on to an oiled baking sheet. Leave to cool and harden.

4 Cover the cooled praline with clear film or put it in a strong plastic bag. Break it into rough pieces by tapping with a rolling pin.

5 If finely ground praline is needed, crush it in a food processor or coffee grinder.

Other flavourings

Coffee

Iced desserts can be made successfully with freshly-made filter coffee or good instant coffee. Strong filter or espresso coffee is preferable for coffee granita, while coffee ice cream can be made with cracked coffee beans. Bring milk or cream to the boil, add the beans and infuse them, then strain the mixture and use the flavoured milk as the basis for the custard in the ice cream. Another way to make coffee ice cream is by blending cold, strong filter coffee or instant coffee dissolved in a very small amount of water with thick custard and cream. While cracked coffee beans give perhaps the best flavour and a pretty speckled finish (after straining) it can be difficult to judge quantities, so this method is more demanding. If too many beans are used or the custard is overcooked, the finished ice cream can be bitter.

Spirits and liqueurs

The addition of a favourite spirit such as brandy, Calvados or whisky to ice cream, gin or vodka to sorbet, or an orange-flavoured liqueur to a fruity granita can lift a simple iced dessert into the realms of gourmet dining. While it is important to add sufficient alcohol to flavour the mixture (bearing in mind that freezing will dull the flavour), it is also vital to note that too much alcohol can prevent the ice cream or sorbet from freezing hard.

Purists or professional ice cream makers test the density and balance of an ice cream before freezing, using a saccharometer, but a beer-making hydrometer may also be used. This enables the level of sugar to liquid to be checked, ensuring satisfactory freezing. The home cook is unlikely to go to these lengths and the best guide when adapting or making up recipes is to taste the mixture before freezing. If it is bland, don't add extra spirit, but pour a little over the ice cream just before serving.

FLAVOURING DURING FREEZING

To add additional flavour and texture, praline, sugared breadcrumbs, crumbled cookies, diced chocolate, diced glacé fruits or brandy-soaked dried fruits can be folded into semi-frozen ice cream. If you are using an ice cream maker, transfer the ice cream to a plastic tub or similar freezerproof container when it is thick, but still soft, before folding in the chosen flavouring. If you are making the ice cream by hand, fold in the flavouring after the second beating.

ABOVE: *Spirits and liqueurs can be used in small quantities to add flavour to ice creams.*

Honey

For a single pot of honey, bees have to visit more than two million flowers. The type of flowers and the time of harvest determine the flavour, colour and texture of the finished honey. You can choose from clover, lavender or heather honey, and cheaper blends are also available that include honey from more than one country. Clear heather honey has the best flavour for making ice cream and tastes especially delicious mixed with goat's milk.

ABOVE: *Alcohol is an excellent flavouring for all iced desserts.*

Using Moulds

There is no need to buy specialist equipment unless you plan to make moulded ice creams on a regular basis or you have a particular favourite. Look through your kitchen cupboards and you may be surprised to find that an item you use regularly or had forgotten about is just the shape you need. Any item not specifically designed to be used for ice cream making should be lined with clear film. Use a generous amount, so that there is enough overlap to cover the exposed surface of the ice cream to stop it drying out in the freezer.

TRANSFORMING EVERYDAY EQUIPMENT

- For rectangular ice cream bombes or terrines, metal loaf tins can be used. Both the 450g | 1lb and the 900g | 2lb sizes are suitable, or you can experiment with the larger, hinged metal pâté tins. Unless tins have a non-stick finish, line them with clear film. If all your loaf tins have sloping sides, don't despair. Simply cut a piece of cardboard the length and height of the tin and use it to make the shape rectangular. Line this with clear film, pushing it carefully into the corners.

- For bombes or cassatas you may have a plastic pudding basin with a lid left over from last year's bought Christmas pudding, or you may have bought such a basin for fridge storage. These make ideal moulds, as the thin plastic conducts the cold well in the freezer and the plastic can be flexed to aid turning out.

- For kulfi, use conical-shaped lolly moulds without their lids or sticks. New disposable plastic cups also work well.

- For individual moulds, old china cups can be lined with clear film. If you can lay your hands on them, the tiny plastic pots with lids used for freezing baby food are ideal.

- New disposable plastic cups or small, well-washed cream cartons that have lids also make good containers. Metal dariole moulds or individual metal steamed pudding moulds can also be used if they are first lined with clear film. This ensures turning out the finished ice.

- If you don't have an ice cream cone mould, make a cardboard cone from an empty cereal packet and cover it with foil. Alternatively, stuff cone shapes made from crumpled foil into cream horn tins so that they become one-third longer.

LEFT: *Specialized bombe, dariole and ring moulds will ensure a professional finish but they can be an expensive piece of kitchen equipment.*

BELOW: *Individual metal steamed-pudding moulds can be used if lined with clear film.*

- If you have used an ordinary glass or china basin, do not dip it in hot water or the mould may break. Simply insert a knife between the clear film and the side of the basin to release the vacuum. Invert the basin on a serving plate, then warm the outside by covering it with a hot dish cloth. Count to 20 and then lift the basin off. Glass and china are poor conductors of heat so will require longer and more gradual warming than metal. When dipping moulds, use hot tap water rather than boiling water from the kettle, which would cause the outside of the ice cream to melt instantly and run over the plate when turned out.

Improvising shaped moulds

Individual ice cream moulds can also be shaped from 2.5–4cm | 1–1½in strips of flexible cardboard which have been wrapped in a layer of foil. These covered strips are folded or curved and then stapled into the desired shape. You might try making hearts, circles or ovals, or fold the edges of the cardboard and make into squares or triangles.

1 Wrap a sheet of foil around a strip of cardboard cut to the desired height.

2 Bend the cardboard into a heart shape, then staple the two ends together.

3 Support the shape on a baking sheet, fill with ice cream that is on the point of setting, then level the surface with a knife and freeze until completely firm.

4 Cut the foil-covered card with scissors and peel it away. Slide a palette knife under the shaped ice cream, lift it on to a serving plate and decorate with fruit or chocolate curls.

ADDING INTEREST TO LAYERS

Ice cream layers in a moulded dessert don't have to be restricted to traditional horizontal lines but can be set at angles by propping up the mould as it freezes. The ice cream can be frozen in one layer to form a triangle or frozen as three layers, each set at opposing angles for a zigzag effect. Terrine or loaf-shaped tins, and square shapes are ideal. Make sure that there is room in the freezer before you begin, as the angled mould and its supports take up quite a lot of space. Bags of frozen vegetables or small boxes of frozen fruit are ideal for wedging the tin at a 45˚ angle. When the first layer is frozen add the next on the opposite side of the mould and wedge in position.

Unmoulding an iced dessert

1 Dip the filled metal or plastic mould into hot water and leave it for a couple of seconds. Lift it out and blot the excess water. If the mould is lined with clear film, carefully insert a knife between the film and the mould to loosen the ice cream.

2 Invert the dessert on a serving plate, lift off the mould and peel away the clear film. If you have difficulty turning out the dessert, try dipping the mould into the hot water for a few seconds more and repeat the process as before.

3 Another way to ease an iced pudding from its mould is to invert it on the serving plate and cover the mould with a clean dish towel which has been dipped in boiling water, and then wrung out. Leave the dish towel in place for a few seconds, and lift off the mould.

Layering and Rippling

For a professional look and a dramatic effect, create different layers of harmonizing ice creams in large or small, rectangular or round moulds. There are plenty of possibilities – just let your imagination take over.

How to layer ices

Simple three-tier ice cream

1 When the first flavour has thickened and is semi-frozen, pour it into a 25 x 7.5 x 7.5cm | 10 x 3 x 3in terrine or loaf tin that has been lined with clear film. Spread it in an even layer and freeze it in the coldest part of the freezer for 1 hour or until firm.

2 Pour in the second layer of semi-frozen ice cream and spread it out evenly. Freeze until firm, then add the final ice cream layer and freeze for 4–5 hours until hard. When ready to serve, turn out the ice cream from the mould, peel off the clear film and cut the terrine into slices, using a warm knife.

Chequerboard

1 Make a two-tier terrine, using two of your favourite ice creams layered in a terrine or straight sided 900g | 2lb loaf tin. Turn out the two-tier terrine on a board and cut it in half lengthways, using a hot knife.

2 Turn one of the halves over to reverse the colour sequence and wrap tightly in clear film to stick them together. Refreeze to harden. To serve, peel away the clear film and slice with a hot knife.

Iced roulade

1 Prepare two quantities of semi-frozen ice cream with flavours that complement each other well. Line a 30 x 23cm | 12 x 9in baking sheet with clear film or waxed paper. Spread one quantity of thick, semi-frozen, flavoured ice cream. Freeze for 20 minutes.

2 Spoon the second batch of semi-frozen ice cream over a second piece of clear film or waxed paper to make a rectangle a little smaller than the first. Freeze for 20 minutes. Carefully place this sheet of ice cream over the first layer, then peel off the clear film or waxed paper.

3 Roll the layered ice cream, as if making a Swiss roll, starting from the longest edge and using the clear film or paper to roll it. Pat the ice cream into a neat cylinder, then wrap it in more clear film. Freeze for several hours, overnight if time permits, until the roll is hard.

4 Peel off the clear film or paper and put the roll on a board. Cut it into thick slices, using a warmed knife.

Classic cassata

This classic Italian iced dessert is traditionally made in a rounded metal mould with a lid. Some think that it is modelled on the dome of the Brunelleschi cathedral in Florence; others believe that the famous dessert was the result of a culinary accident when cream and wine were accidentally spilled into a soldier's metal helmet which was being stored in a chilly cave. Whatever its true origins, cassata is traditionally served in Italy at weddings and Easter celebrations and comprises two or three layers of ice cream, depending on the size of the mould in which it is made. If you don't have a metal mould, a plastic or thick glass pudding basin can be used instead.

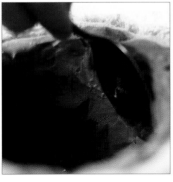

1 Line a 1.2 litre | 2 pint | 5 cup pudding basin with clear film. Line it with a 2cm | ¾in thick layer of semi-frozen strawberry ice cream, using the back of a metal spoon to press the ice cream against the sides and bottom of the basin. Cover and freeze for 1–2 hours or until the ice cream lining is firm.

2 Again using the back of a metal spoon, press chocolate ice cream on to the strawberry ice cream in the mould to make a second 2cm | ¾in thick layer of chocolate ice cream against the frozen strawberry layer. Leave a space in the centre. Cover and freeze for 1–2 hours more or until the chocolate ice cream is firm.

3 Pack the centre of the mould with tutti frutti ice cream and smooth the top. Cover and freeze the dessert overnight until firm. Dip the mould in hot water for 10 seconds, insert a knife between the clear film and the basin to loosen the cassata, then invert it on to a serving plate. Lift off the basin and peel away the clear film before decorating the dessert with glacé fruits or chocolate caraque. Serve in wedges.

Individual bombes

1 Line four individual metal moulds with clear film, then press a 1cm | ½in layer of dark chocolate ice cream over the bottom and sides of each mould, smoothing the ice cream with the back of a teaspoon. Cover and freeze for 30 minutes or until the ice cream is firm.

2 Add a scoop of vanilla ice cream to the centre of each lined mould and insert a brandy-soaked prune or cherry into the middle. Smooth the surface, cover and freeze for 4 hours until firm.

3 Dip the filled moulds into a roasting tin filled with hot water for 2 seconds. Invert the moulds on to serving plates and quickly remove the tins and clear film.

4 Decorate the top and sides of each individual bombe with long sweeping lines of piped white chocolate. Serve immediately.

How to ripple ices

This dramatic and eye-catching effect is surprisingly easy to achieve, using ice creams and sauces in contrasting colours, which are lightly swirled together while the ice cream is semi-frozen.

Flavoured ice cream

Choose softly set ice cream that is too soft to scoop but thick enough to hold its shape. The colours should be markedly different for the most dramatic effect.

Sauces

Marble a chocolate, toffee or fruit sauce through ice cream that is on the verge of setting. Be careful with toffee sauces as they can dissolve into the ice cream, so losing the effect.

Raspberry ripple ice cream

Fruit purée

Puréed and sieved fruit purées can be used unsweetened but can taste rather icy. It is better to mix them with a thick sugar syrup before swirling them with semi-frozen ice cream.

Jam

For the easiest rippled ice cream of all, use softly set extra fruit jam straight from the jar. You can use firmer jams, but they will need to be mixed with a little boiling water to soften before being used. Make sure the jam is cold when you use it, or it will melt the ice cream. Any fruit jam can be used but the contrast of berry fruits looks the most attractive.

LEFT: *Use softly set jam for ice creams.*

1 Make the vanilla ice cream by hand or churn it in an ice cream maker until it is thick but too soft to scoop.

2 Mix 75g|3oz|6 tbsp caster sugar with 60ml|4 tbsp water in a pan. Heat until the sugar has dissolved, then boil for 3 minutes until syrupy, but not coloured. Cool slightly. Purée 250g|9oz|1½ cups fresh raspberries in a food processor or blender then press through a sieve over a bowl. Stir in the syrup and chill well.

3 Add alternate spoonfuls of the soft, partially frozen vanilla ice cream and the chilled raspberry syrup to a 1 litre|1¼ pint|4 cup plastic tub or similar freezerproof container. Don't be alarmed if the contrasting layers look a little messy to begin with.

4 Stir through the syrup and ice cream two or three times to create a rippled effect. Freeze.

CLASSIC COMBINATIONS

Ripple one of the basic recipes in this book with one of your own favourite flavours. Use the same basic technique as for raspberry ripple.

Mixed berry swirl – strawberry ice cream with raspberry syrup.

Coffee toffee swirl – dark classic coffee ice cream swirled with a rich toffee sauce.

Double chocolate – smooth dark chocolate ice cream rippled with smooth white chocolate ice cream.

Apricot and orange ripple – orange and yogurt ice rippled with apricot sauce.

Creamy toffee ripple – rich toffee sauce rippled through creamy vanilla ice cream.

Raspberry ripple – try the home-made version made with the very best of ingredients for a truly timeless classic.

Marbling ice cream

Although very similar to the technique used when making a rippled ice cream, marbling creates softer, less defined swirls. The same combinations of ice cream and syrup, sauce or purée can be used as for making rippled ice creams, but the softer effect is achieved by mixing together more thoroughly.

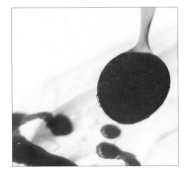

1 To achieve this effect, spoon alternate layers of partially frozen ice cream into a plastic tub or similar freezerproof container. Drizzle coloured liquid flavouring or syrup, over each layer, using a spoon.

2 Pass the handle of a wooden spoon through the ice cream and liquid flavouring five or six times to produce a lightly marbled effect. Freeze the ice cream for 4–5 hours or overnight, until firm.

COOK'S TIP *Soft marbled ice cream need only be lightly swirled with the end of a spoon to create the required effect. Choose a coloured liquid flavouring that complements the base ice cream in colour and taste.*

ABOVE: *A single scoop of marbled ice cream.*

SECRETS OF SUCCESS

- Line the mould with clear film so that it is easy to remove the frozen dessert.

- Choose flavours that contrast or complement each other, such as dark chocolate with pistachio, or vanilla and strawberry.

- Freeze ice cream after each layer has been added so that soft mixtures do not merge together. That way, the finished dessert will have well-defined layers.

- Make sure that the colours of the ice cream are in harmony, but are strong enough to be visible.

- Freeze the mould thoroughly after layering, preferably overnight, so that the layers will not separate when the ice cream is sliced.

- Dip the mould in hot water for 10–15 seconds so that the dessert will turn out easily. Peel off the clear film and use a knife dipped into warm water for slicing.

Ice Cream Lollies

Everyone loves an ice lolly, especially children, and these are particularly delicious. Making your own is also a good idea because you know exactly what ingredients they contain.

SINGLE FLAVOURS

Milk maid
The simplest lolly of all. Made with full-fat milk poured into moulds and frozen until firm. Ideal as a first lolly for small children.

Orange refresher
Another very easy lolly, made by simply filling moulds with freshly squeezed orange juice or juice from a carton. The flavours can be varied, try tropical fruit juices, apple, cranberry juice or mixed juices.

Strawberry yogurt
Mix a 150ml | ¼ pint | ⅔ cup carton of strawberry yogurt with the same quantity of full-fat milk. Stir in 10ml | 2 tsp strawberry milkshake powder, pour into lolly moulds and top up with extra milk if needed.

Banana custard
Mash two small ripe bananas with 5ml | 1 tsp lemon juice, then stir with a small carton of ready-made custard. Add enough full-fat milk to fill the moulds.

ABOVE: *Lolly moulds have handles to hold the ice lollies.*

MULTICOLOURED LOLLIES

Traffic light lollies
Fill each lolly mould one-third full with sieved strawberry purée, then freeze until hard. Add a second layer, the same width as the first, of orange juice. Freeze that until hard, then top up with orange juice tinted with a little blue food colouring so that it goes green. Freeze until hard.

Rainbow lollies
Experiment with colour combinations. Fruit purées, sieved and sweetened with a little sugar if very sharp, work very well. Try mango, kiwi fruit, strawberry and blackberry, for example. Alternatively, create layers of different colours by tinting orange juice with drops of edible food colouring. A few drops of green will turn orange juice blue; a little blue will change it to green; red will intensify the orange colour. A combination of fruit purées and tinted juice also works well, and for creamy-tasting lollies you can use different flavours of sorbet or ice cream. Let your imagination run wild, but always use sorbet or ice cream that is partially frozen and do make sure to freeze each coloured layer until it is hard before adding the next layer or the colours will bleed into each other.

TWO TONE AND DOUBLE DECKER LOLLIES

Summer sunset

Pour a layer of sieved strawberry or raspberry purée into lolly moulds, and freeze. Top up with orange juice and freeze until solid. Add a little vodka or tequila for an adult version.

In the pink

Slide a strawberry slice down the side of each mould then half-fill with partially frozen home-made strawberry ice cream. Freeze until firm, then top with home-made strawberry sorbet, and freeze.

SWIRLED AND RIPPLED LOLLIES

Night and day

Add alternate spoonfuls of semi-frozen white and dark chocolate ice cream to lolly moulds. Lightly mix them together with a fine metal skewer for a swirled effect and freeze until solid.

Banana and raspberry ripple

Fill the lolly moulds with alternate spoonfuls of semi-frozen banana ice cream and raspberry syrup. Lightly stir them with a fine metal skewer and freeze until solid.

COATED AND DIPPED LOLLIES

Double choc

Fill moulds with partially frozen home-made chocolate ice cream, freeze until hard then remove from the moulds and coat the top half of each lolly with finely grated dark chocolate.

Strawberry sprinkle

Fill moulds with partially frozen home-made strawberry ice cream, freeze until hard, then remove from the moulds. Drizzle melted white chocolate over the top portion of each lolly, then sprinkle this with pastel-coloured sugar strands. For a simpler version, press the sugar strands straight on to ice cream.

FREEZING LOLLIES

Lolly moulds come in various sizes, some enable you to make six small lollies; others have space for four large ones. Pour in the mixture to come almost to the top, then press in the lolly handles. Freeze for at least 6 hours or overnight until hard.

COOK'S TIP *If you don't have any lolly moulds or want to make lots of lollies for a children's party, use small disposable plastic cups or a deep ice cube tray. Empty mini pots which originally contained fromage frais can also be used, provided they are thoroughly washed. Lolly sticks can be saved and recycled, or you can improvise with a length of dowelling bought from your local DIY store. Cut it into suitable lengths, sand it well so that the wood is completely smooth, and wash the sticks thoroughly before use.*

Turning lollies out

Hold the rounded ends of the moulds under running hot water or stand the moulds in a bowl of hot water. This should not be so deep that the water comes up to the handles – two-thirds of the way up is ideal. Count to 15, then flex the handles and lift out the lollies.

Ice cream petits fours

1 Arrange a toasted almond, hazelnut or brandy-soaked cherry in each of the sections of an ice cube tray. Cover with thick ice cream that is partially frozen. Level the top of each cube with a palette knife and freeze until solid.

2 Pour just-boiled water from the kettle over the upturned ice cube tray, drain, then flex the tray to release the ice cream cubes. Arrange these on a small fine-meshed cooling rack set over a plate or baking sheet.

3 Spoon melted chocolate over the cubes, covering the tops and sides, and let it set. Turn each cube over and coat the underside and any gaps. Return to the freezer for a minute or two, then arrange on the inverted lid of a plastic container. Decorate with any remaining chocolate. Fit the upturned container and freeze until required. Allow to soften for a few minutes before serving.

Ice cream kebabs

1 Pour a little of your favourite fruit ice cream into each section of an ice cube tray, freeze until solid, then turn out and thread on to hot metal skewers, leaving a little space between the ice cream cubes. Quickly put the kebabs in the freezer so that the ice cream stays hard.

2 When you are ready to serve, arrange two skewers on each serving plate. Decorate each ice cream cube with a slice of strawberry or kiwi fruit and serve with Melba sauce.

COOK'S TIP *Vanilla or chocolate ice creams are perhaps the best choice for these dainty petits fours, but cashew and orange, pistachio, coconut or orange and yogurt are also delicious. Cover the ice cream cubes in batches of five or seven and work quickly so they don't melt before they are completely covered with chocolate. Using an upturned plastic box for storage in the freezer protects them from any knocks, and makes it easy to transfer them to plates for serving. Warm the skewers by dipping them in water that has recently boiled, or by holding them in an oven mitt and warming them over the flame on a gas hob so that they pierce the hard ice cream easily. Kebabs can also be made from a solid block of ice cream which has been cut into cubes.*

Baskets, Biscuits and Cones

Not only beautiful to look at, these sensational edible containers are easy to make and bound to impress your guests. They are the ultimate stylish and professional presentation.

How to make baskets

Spun sugar baskets

These impressive baskets look stunning filled with ice cream or upturned and placed over a single scoop of ice cream to form a cage and arranged in the centre of a large white dinner plate. Use an oiled soup ladle instead of oranges for slightly flatter baskets, and loosen with the tip of a small knife before removing. Add rich colour by decorating the plate with tiny clusters of blueberries, a few raspberries and a sprig or two of redcurrants or any combination of summer fruits. Dust lightly with icing sugar for the final effect.

MAKES SIX

INGREDIENTS

3 ORANGES, to serve as moulds

a little OIL for greasing

250g | 9oz | generous 1 cup GRANULATED SUGAR

75ml | 5 tbsp WATER

VANILLA ICE CREAM and
FRESH SUMMER FRUITS, to serve

1 Smooth squares of foil over three oranges and brush lightly with oil. Put the granulated sugar and water in a saucepan and heat gently, without stirring, until the sugar has completely dissolved. Increase the heat and boil the syrup until it turns golden and starts to caramelize.

2 Take the pan off the heat and plunge the bottom of it into a bowl of cold water to prevent the caramel from overbrowning. Allow the caramel to cool for 15–30 seconds, stirring it gently until it starts to thicken, then lift the pan out of the water.

3 Hold a foil-wrapped orange over the pan and quickly drizzle caramel from a dessertspoon over half the orange, making squiggly lines and gradually building up layers to make the basket shape. Leave the caramel to set and make a second and third basket in the same way. Warm the caramel when it gets too stiff to drizzle.

4 Ease the foil off the first orange. Carefully peel the foil away and put the finished sugar basket on a lightly oiled baking sheet. Repeat with the remaining baskets, then make three more in the same way, reheating the caramel as needed and adding a little boiling water if it gets too thick to drizzle.

5 Use the baskets on the day you make them, filling them with vanilla ice cream and summer fruits and adding a dusting of sifted icing sugar. The baskets are extremely fragile, so scoop the ice cream on to a plate or baking sheet first and lower it carefully into each basket with the aid of two forks.

Chocolate tulips

These easy-to-make tulip baskets take only minutes to prepare and can then be set aside to harden. Fill with one large scoop of ice cream and decorate with blueberries and halved strawberries, or fill with tiny scoops of ice cream shaped with a melon baller and decorate with tiny chocolate shapes.

VARIATIONS *Any of the chocolate basket ideas suggested here are a perfect way of setting off your favourite chocolate, coffee or vanilla ice cream. You do not have to use dark chocolate to make the baskets – Belgian white or milk chocolate work just as well.*

1 Using the back of a teaspoon, spread 175g|6oz melted dark chocolate over six 13cm|5in circles of non-stick baking parchment, taking it almost, but not completely, to the edge, and giving it a swirly, wave-like edge.

2 Drape each paper circle, chocolate side outwards, over an upturned glass tumbler set on a baking sheet. Ease the paper into soft pleats and leave the baskets in a cool place to set. When ready to serve, lift the baskets off the glasses and carefully peel away the paper.

A large chocolate bowl

3 Chill well until set, then carefully peel away the foil and place the bowl on a plate. Store in the fridge until ready to fill with ice cream.

COOK'S TIP *This bowl can be made in any size. Small ones are perfect for individual portions, while larger bowls can serve up to four. Make it thicker than the other bowls and don't fill it too full or the weight of the ice cream might cause the chocolate to crack.*

1 Smooth a double thickness of foil into a suitably sized mixing bowl or basin, so that it takes on the shape of the container. Carefully lift the foil out of the bowl.

2 Spoon melted chocolate into the bottom of the foil bowl. Spread it to an even, fairly thick layer, taking it over the base and sides with the back of a spoon or a pastry brush.

Individual chocolate cups

3 Fill each of the set chocolate cups with parfait. Chill again in the freezer, then carefully peel away the paper from each cup. Using a palette knife to transfer each filled cup to a plate, decorate them with a light dusting of sifted cocoa and serve.

COOK'S TIP *When melting chocolate, it is important that the chocolate isn't overheated or allowed to come into contact with steam or small amounts of moisture, as these will cause it to stiffen or "seize". Make sure that the base of the bowl doesn't touch the water and don't allow the water to boil.*

1 Cut six 30 x 15cm|12 x 6in strips of non-stick baking parchment. Fold each strip in half lengthways, roll into a circle and fit it inside a 7.5cm|3in plain biscuit cutter to make a collar. Secure with tape. Ease the biscuit cutter away and make five more collars, leaving the last collar inside the cutter. Place on a baking sheet.

2 Melt 250g/9oz dark chocolate in a heatproof bowl over a pan of hot water. Brush chocolate evenly over the base and sides of the paper collar, supported by the biscuit cutter, and make the top edge jagged. Carefully lift off the biscuit cutter and slide over the next paper collar. Make six cups and leave to set.

How to make biscuits

Tuile biscuits

These classic French biscuits are named after the similarly shaped roof tiles found on many old French homes. Made with ground and crushed almonds, these biscuits are shaped by being draped over a rolling pin as they cool, but cigar-shaped rolls or cones are also made.

SERVES SIX

INGREDIENTS

little OIL, for greasing

50g | 2oz | ¼ cup UNSALTED BUTTER

75g | 3oz | ¾ cup FLAKED ALMONDS

2 MEDIUM EGG WHITES

75g | 3oz | 6 tbsp CASTER SUGAR

50g | 2oz | ½ cup PLAIN FLOUR, sifted

RIND of ½ ORANGE, finely grated plus 10ml/2 tsp JUICE

SIFTED ICING SUGAR, to decorate

1 Preheat the oven to 200°C | 400°F | Gas 6. Lightly brush a wooden rolling pin with oil, and line two large baking sheets with non-stick baking parchment. Melt the butter in a saucepan and set it aside. Preheat the grill. Spread out the flaked almonds on a baking sheet and lightly brown under the grill. Leave to cool, then finely grind half; crush the remainder roughly with your fingertips.

2 Put the egg whites and sugar in a bowl and lightly fork them together. Sift in the flour, stir gently to mix, then fold in the melted butter, then the orange rind and juice. Fold in the finely ground nuts.

3 Drop six teaspoons of the mixture on to one of the lined baking sheets, spacing them well apart. Spread the biscuits into thin circles and sprinkle lightly with the crushed nuts. Bake in the oven for 5 minutes until lightly browned around the edges.

COOK'S TIP *It is important to transfer the biscuits to the rolling pin as quickly as possible. As the biscuits cool they will set and become crisp and it will not be possible to shape them.*

4 Loosen one of the biscuits with a palette knife and drape it over the rolling pin. Shape the remaining biscuits in the same way. Leave for 5 minutes to set while baking a second tray of biscuits. Continue baking and shaping biscuits until all the mixture has been used. Dust with icing sugar and serve with ice cream.

Cigarettes russes

These biscuits are smaller and rolled more tightly than tuiles, but can be made using the same recipe. Omit the nuts, orange rind and juice and add 5ml | 1 tsp vanilla essence. Make 2–3 biscuits at a time, each time using 10ml | 2 tsp of the mixture spread into a thin circle. The mixture makes 15 cigarettes russes.

Bake the biscuits until they are golden around the edges, then turn them over and wrap them around lightly oiled wooden spoon handles.

Brandy snaps

Traditionally rolled into fat cigar shapes, these crisp, lacy biscuits can also be made into tiny petits fours or even baskets – all perfect accompaniments to home-made ice cream.

MAKES 32

INGREDIENTS

a little OIL, for greasing

115g|4oz|½ cup UNSALTED BUTTER

115g|4oz|generous ½ cup CASTER SUGAR

115g|4oz|⅓ cup GOLDEN SYRUP

115g|4oz|1 cup PLAIN FLOUR

5ml|1 tsp GROUND GINGER

15ml|1 tbsp LEMON JUICE

15ml|1 tbsp BRANDY

COOK'S TIP *Brandy snaps can be made the day before being served. Store them covered with greaseproof paper in a cool, dry place. They can also be frozen. Pack in layers in a rigid plastic box, interleaved with greaseproof paper.*

1 Preheat the oven to 190°C| 375°F|Gas 5. Lightly oil the handles of two or three wooden spoons (or more if you have them). Line two baking sheets with non-stick baking parchment. Put the butter, sugar and syrup into a medium saucepan and heat gently, stirring occasionally until the butter has melted.

2 Take the pan off the heat and sift in the flour and ginger. Mix well until smooth, then stir in the lemon juice and brandy.

4 Quickly roll each brandy snap around the handle of an oiled wooden spoon and put join-side downwards on a wire rack to cool. Leave to set for 1 minute, then remove the spoon from the first biscuit and shape the others on the tray in the same way, by which time the second batch of biscuits will probably be ready.

3 Drop four teaspoons of the mixture on to the lined baking sheets, spacing them well apart. Cook for 5–6 minutes, until they are pale brown, bubbling and the edges are just darkening. Take the tray of biscuits out of the oven, leave them to stand for 15–30 seconds to set slightly, then loosen the biscuits with a palette knife.

CHOCOLATE SNAPS

For chocolate-flavoured brandy snaps substitute 15g|½oz|2 tbsp of sifted cocoa powder for 15g|½oz|2 tbsp of the flour. Do not use drinking-chocolate powder as this has added sugar and dried milk powder.

Mini biscuits for petits fours

1 Spoon half teaspoons of the basic brandy snap mixture on to lined baking sheets. Bake until golden brown, then shape around oiled wooden satay sticks or metal kebab skewers. Work quickly, as the small biscuits will cool rapidly.

2 For mini cornets, shape the biscuits by wrapping them around the ends of oiled cream horn tins or large piping tubes. Remove the tins or piping tubes and dip the ends of the biscuits into melted white or dark chocolate, if liked.

Brandy snap baskets

1 Drop 15ml|1 tbsp of the basic brandy snap mixture on to a lined baking sheet, spread it to a circle and cook for 6–7 minutes. Cool for a few seconds until firm enough to remove. Quickly lift the biscuit and drape it, textured side outwards, over an orange that has been lightly brushed with oil.

2 Flute the edges by easing the biscuit into folds with your fingertips. Leave to cool. As soon as it has set, lift it off the orange.

COOK'S TIP *These baskets are best made one at a time. They cook quickly and are shaped in a couple of minutes.*

How to make cones

Chocolate cones

1 Line the inside of as many cream horn tins as you need with non-stick baking parchment so that it sticks out of the ends of the tins slightly and the ends overlap inside.

2 Brush the inside of each paper cone with melted chocolate, chill for 15 minutes, then brush over a second layer of chocolate. Chill well, then fill with softly set ice cream. Stand the filled cream horn tins in mugs to keep them upright or wedge them in a plastic tub, using crumpled kitchen paper or foil to keep them upright. Freeze until firm.

3 Carefully pull the chocolate cones out of the tins, holding them by the paper, then gently peel the paper away. Lay the filled cones on individual plates and decorate with chocolate curls. Dust each plate with sifted cocoa.

Tuile ice cream cones

1 Use the basic recipe for tuiles, to make ten lacy ice cream cones on wooden moulds. They are extremely fragile so fill with care. These cones are best eaten on the day they are made. Make two cones at a time, using 15ml|1 tbsp of mixture per cone. Spread thinly into 10cm|4in circles, sprinkle with nuts and bake at 180°C|350°F|Gas 4 for 5 minutes, until golden around the edges.

2 Have ready an oiled, wooden ice cream cone mould. Loosen a biscuit, using a palette knife, turn it over and put it on a clean, folded dish towel supported on the palm of your left hand. Lay the cone mould on top and wrap the biscuit around it to form the cone shape. Repeat with the second biscuit, then repeat with the remaining mixture.

Mini cones

1 Using about 10ml|2 tsp of biscuit mixture each time, make two well-spaced mounds on a lined baking sheet. Don't bother to spread them flat. Bake for 4 minutes until the biscuits are starting to brown around the edges.

2 Let the biscuits cool slightly, then loosen them with a palette knife, turn them over and carefully roll them around cream horn tins (see Cook's Tip).

COOK'S TIP *If you like, you can make cream horn tins bigger by stuffing them with crumpled foil until they are about one third longer. Brush them lightly with oil before using them as moulds. Wooden ice cream cone moulds are available from specialist cook shops or by mail order.*

Transforming bought cones

1 Liven up ready-made cones by dipping the tops in a little melted dark, white or milk chocolate and then sprinkling with chopped toasted hazelnuts, toasted flaked almonds or roughly chopped pistachios.

2 Coat the rims of cones in melted white chocolate and sprinkle with grated dark chocolate or curls.

3 For children's parties, stud cones with jewel-like arrangements of sugar diamonds or sugar flowers, sticking them on with dots of melted white chocolate. Or dip the rim of each cone into melted white chocolate, then into pastel-coloured sugar sprinkles.

Making Ice Bowls

These impressive ice bowls make a wonderful dinner party centrepiece. They are incredibly easy to make and need no specialist equipment – but make sure you have enough room in your freezer!

A decorated ice bowl

1 You will need two pyrex or plastic bowls that will fit one inside the other leaving a gap of about 2–2.5cm | ¾–1in. Tape the bowls together, using parcel tape and making sure that the gap between them is constant all the way round.

2 Put the double bowl on a plate to catch any drips. Carefully fill the gap between the bowls with cooled boiled water. It should come almost to the top. For a more frosted look, use cold water straight from the tap.

3 Slide slices of citrus fruits, small flowers, herbs or spices into the water between the bowls, using a skewer to tease them into place if necessary. Freeze overnight until hard.

4 To unmould the ice bowl, peel off the tape. Place the bowls in a washing up bowl half filled with hot water and pour a little hot water into the smaller bowl. Count to 30 then lift the bowls out of the water, pour the water out of the smaller bowl and loosen the ice bowl with a thin, round-bladed knife.

5 Lift out the inner bowl, turn out the ice bowl and put it on a large plate. Decorate the plate with a few extra flowers or leaves and fill the bowl with ice cream. If you are serving it as part of a buffet you could unmould it ahead of time, fill it with ice cream and return it to the freezer until ready to serve. Decorate the serving plate just before taking to the table.

BEAUTIFUL BOWLS

• In summer there are many edible garden flowers and herbs that can be used to decorate ice bowls. Try pansies and chives with rosemary and sweet cicely, or strawberry fruit, flowers and leaves for a very pretty effect. Fill the bowl with berry sorbet, or vanilla and strawberry ice cream.

• For a fresh citrus look, use orange, lemon and lime slices to make the ice bowl, adding a few sliced kumquats, if available. Decorate the serving plate with nasturtiums or calendula marigold flowers and fill with scoops of ice cream or sorbet in complementary colours.

• Celebrate the festive season with an ice bowl decorated with an arrangement of bay leaves and cranberries made to look like sprigs of holly. Add cinnamon sticks, whole star anise and a few orange slices too. Fill with a rich dairy ice cream, rum and raisin or a tutti-frutti ice cream.

Classic Ice Cream Sauces

No ice cream sundae would be complete without one of these popular sauces. For convenience, they can all be made in advance and stored in the fridge until needed, and can be served hot or cold, as preferred.

How to make sauces

Chocolate sauce

Rich, dark and irresistible. Pour the warm or cold sauce over vanilla or milk chocolate ice cream or serve with an ice cream sundae made with your favourite flavours.

MAKES 400ml | 14fl oz | 1⅔ cups

INGREDIENTS

25g | 1oz | 2 tbsp BUTTER

25g | 1oz | 2 tbsp CASTER SUGAR

30ml | 2 tbsp GOLDEN SYRUP

200g | 7oz LUXURY PLAIN COOKING CHOCOLATE

150ml | ¼ pint | ⅔ cup SEMI-SKIMMED MILK

45ml | 3 tbsp DOUBLE CREAM

1 Mix the butter, caster sugar and syrup in a saucepan. Break the chocolate into pieces and add it to the mixture. Heat very gently, stirring occasionally, until the chocolate has melted.

2 Gradually stir in the milk and cream and bring just to the boil, stirring constantly until smooth. Serve hot or cool, refrigerate and reheat when required.

Butterscotch sauce

Smooth and glossy, this creamy toffee sauce is extremely rich. It is delicious with vanilla, coffee or yogurt ice creams. Once made, it can be stored in the fridge for up to 4 days.

MAKES 475ml | 16fl oz | 2 cups

INGREDIENTS

200g | 7oz | 1 cup CASTER SUGAR

45ml | 3 tbsp each COLD WATER and BOILING WATER

75g | 3oz | 6 tbsp BUTTER

150ml | ¼ pint | ⅔ cup DOUBLE CREAM

3 Standing as far back as possible, and protecting your hand with an oven glove, add the 45ml/3 tbsp boiling water to the caramel mixture, which will splutter and spit. Add the butter and tilt the pan to mix the ingredients together. Leave to cool for 5 minutes.

COOK'S TIP *Don't be tempted to stir the sugar syrup when it is boiling or you may find that the sugar will crystallize and solidify. If this happens, the mixture cannot be retrieved. You will have to throw it away and begin again.*

1 Put the sugar and 45ml | 3 tbsp cold water into a saucepan and heat very gently, without stirring, until all the sugar has dissolved.

2 Bring the mixture to the boil and boil until the sugar starts to turn golden. Quickly take the pan off the heat and immediately plunge the bottom of the pan into cold water to prevent the sugar from overbrowning.

4 Gradually stir in the cream and mix well. Pour into a jug and serve warm or cool.

Melba sauce

Of all the classic ice cream sauces, this is perhaps the best known. It is very easy, requires no cooking and is delicious served with scoops of vanilla ice cream and sliced ripe peaches. Some versions of this sauce are cooked and thickened with cornflour, but this simple version is by far the best.

MAKES 200ml | 7fl oz | scant 1 cup

INGREDIENTS

250g | 9oz | 1¼ cups fresh or thawed FROZEN RASPBERRIES

30ml | 2 tbsp ICING SUGAR

1 Purée the raspberries in a food processor or blender until smooth.

2 Pour the purée into a sieve set over a bowl. Press the fruit through the sieve and discard the seeds that remain behind in the sieve. Sift in the icing sugar, mix well and chill until required.

USING RIPE FRUIT

This is a wonderful way of using up very soft ripe raspberries. If they are particularly soft, don't purée them first; check them over, then simply press through a sieve with the aid of a wooden spoon.

Apricot Sauce

Delicious with vanilla ice cream, this fruity sauce is a good way of persuading children to eat fruit without realizing what they are doing.

MAKES 350ml | 12fl oz | 1½ cups

INGREDIENTS

200g | 7oz | scant 1 cup READY-TO-EAT DRIED APRICOTS

450ml | ¾ pint | scant 2 cups WATER

25g | 1oz | 2 tbsp CASTER SUGAR

VARIATION *The apricots can also be poached in apple juice or a mixture of half apple juice and half water.*

1 Put the apricots in a saucepan and add the water and sugar. Cover and leave to simmer for 10 minutes until the apricots are tender and plump. Leave to cool.

2 Tip the mixture into a blender or food processor and process to a smooth purée. Scrape into a bowl and chill until ready to serve.

Combining sauces

Spoon a little Melba sauce over half a serving plate, then spoon apricot sauce over the other half. Tilt the plate very gently, first in one direction, then the other, to swirl the edges of the sauce together. Add the ice cream and decorate with sprigs of mint.

INSTANT DESSERTS

Serving plain ice cream with a combination of sauces is a very quick and easy way to produce an exciting dessert. Sauces that contrast in colour or texture are very attractive when used together but avoid using flavours that are not complementary.

COOK'S TIP *Sauces that contrast with each other can be rippled or swirled in exactly the same way as rippling ice cream. Ice cream is then placed on the top.*

Toppings and Decorations

Complete the simplest dish of beautifully scooped ice cream or a party-style sundae with one of these professional looking decorations and you will be sure to impress your dinner guests.

How to make decorations

Plain chocolate caraque

1 Using a palette knife or the back of a spoon spread melted dark chocolate over a marble slab or cheese board, or an offcut of kitchen work surface, to a depth of about 5mm|¼in. Leave in a cool place to set.

2 Draw a long, fine-bladed cook's knife across the chocolate at a 45° angle, using a see-saw action to pare away long curls. If the chocolate is too soft, put it in the fridge for 5 minutes or in a cold place for 15 minutes. Do not overchill.

Piped chocolate shapes

Spoon a little melted dark chocolate into a paper piping bag and snip off the tip. Pipe squiggly shapes, stars, hearts, butterflies, musical notes or even initials on to a lined baking sheet. Peel off when cool and chill until required.

Two-tone caraque

1 Spoon alternate lines of melted white and dark chocolate over a marble slab or cheese board, or an offcut of work surface and spread lightly so that all the chocolate is the same height. Leave to cool and harden.

2 Pare away long, thin curls of chocolate with a fine-bladed cook's knife in the same way that you do when making plain chocolate caraque.

Chocolate rose leaves

Brush melted dark chocolate, as evenly as possible, over the underside of clean, dry rose leaves. Avoid brushing over the edges. Put the leaf onto a non-stick parchment-lined baking sheet and leave in a cool place to set. Carefully peel each leaf away and chill until required.

Simple chocolate curls

Holding a bar of dark, white or milk chocolate over a plate, pare curls away from the edge of the bar, using a swivel-blade vegetable peeler. Lift the pared curls carefully with a flat blade or a palette knife and arrange as desired.

COOK'S TIP *If the chocolate used for decoration is not at the right temperature the curls will either be too brittle or won't hold their shape. Set the chocolate aside at room temperature for 20 minutes before working with it.*

How to make dipped fruits

Fruit looks and tastes fabulous when half dipped in melted dark or white chocolate. Choose from tiny strawberries (still with their green hulls attached), tiny clusters of green or red grapes, physalis or cherries, with their stalks. It can also look very effective if you dip half the fruits in dark chocolate and the remainder in white chocolate. Leave the fruits to set on a baking sheet lined with non-stick baking parchment.

Caramel-dipped fruits

For a more unusual fruit decoration for ice cream dishes, half-dip peeled physalis, whole strawberries or cherries (with the stalks intact) into the warm syrup, then leave to cool and harden on an oiled baking sheet.

COOK'S TIP *Always carefully select fruit used for decoration and check that the fruit is perfect and free of any bruising as this will quickly spoil the decoration. Wipe them over with a damp cloth to remove any dust. A more even effect can be achieved if the stalks are still firmly attached to the fruit.*

Caramel shapes

The caramel used for making baskets is also suitable for making fancy shapes to decorate ice cream sundaes. Instead of drizzling the caramel on to foil-covered oranges, drizzle shapes such as treble clefs, graduated zigzags, spirals, curly scribbles, initials, stars or hearts on to a lightly oiled baking sheet. Vary the sizes, from small decorations about 5cm|2in long to larger 10cm|4in long shapes.

Using coloured chocolate

1 Pipe random lines of melted dark chocolate over a piece of non-stick baking parchment. Overpipe with piped white chocolate. Using pink liquid food colouring, tint a little of the melted white chocolate.

2 Pipe a third layer of chocolate squiggles, this time in pink, over the dark and white layers. Chill in the fridge until set.

3 Break the coloured shapes into jagged fragments of varying sizes and stick them into ice cream to decorate. They look particularly good on top of ice cream sundaes.

Frosted flowers

1 Lightly beat an egg white, then brush a very thin layer over edible flowers such as pansies, violas, nasturtiums, tiny rose buds or petals. Herb flowers can also be used, as can strawberries, seedless grapes or cherries.

2 Sprinkle the flower or fruit with caster sugar and leave to dry on a large plate. Use on the day of making.

Citrus curls

1 Using a zester, pare the rind of an orange, lemon or lime, removing just the coloured rind of the skin and leaving the bitter white pith on the fruit.

2 Dust the citrus curls with a little caster sugar and use them to sprinkle over citrus-based ices such as lemon sorbet.

Corkscrews

1 Use a canelle knife to pare long strips of orange, lemon or lime rind. The strips should be as long as possible and very narrow.

2 Twist the strips of rind tightly around cocktail sticks so that they curl into corkscrews. Slide the sticks out and hang the corkscrew curls over the edge of ice cream dishes.

Meringue dainties

1 Make a meringue mixture using 2 eggs and 115g|4oz|generous ½ cup caster sugar. Spoon it into a large piping bag fitted with either a small plain 5mm|¼ in or a 9mm|⅜in nozzle.

2 Pipe heart shapes, zigzags, shooting stars or geometric shapes on to baking sheets lined with non-stick baking parchment.

3 Sprinkle the shapes lightly with caster sugar and bake at low heat until they are firm enough to be lifted off the paper easily. Cool, then store in a cake tin for up to 1 week or until required.

Decorative effects with sauces

Spooning sauces over ice cream is a quick and simple method of decorating ices and can look particularly pretty over ice cream sundaes, but sauces can also be piped in decorative shapes and patterns or used to create elaborate or dramatic backdrops against which to display your favourite ice creams.

Creating teardrops

1 Spoon a little Melba sauce over the base of a plate, tilt to cover then pipe or spoon small dots of unwhipped double cream around the edge of the plate.

2 Draw a skewer or cocktail stick through the dots to form teardrops. Scoop the ice cream into the centre of the plate.

Feathering

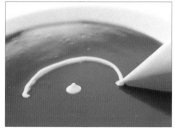

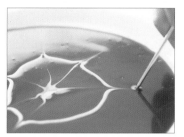

Piping zigzag lines

1 Spoon a little chocolate or butterscotch sauce over the base of a plate, then pipe a central dot and one or more circles of melted white chocolate or double cream on the sauce, starting at the centre and working outwards.

2 Draw a skewer or cocktail stick in lines from the centre of the plate to the rim, like the spokes of a wheel. Or mark lines in alternate directions for a spider's web effect.

Arrange scoops of ice cream on a plate. Spoon a little cooled chocolate sauce into a greaseproof piping bag, snip the tip, and pipe long zigzag lines over the plate and ice cream. For added effect dust with a little sifted cocoa.

Piped border

Decorative squiggles

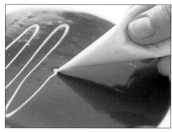

1 Pipe a swirly border of sieved strawberry or apricot jam around the edge of a plate. Alternatively, use melted white or dark chocolate and leave chocolate to set.

2 Using the jam or chocolate as a border, flood the centre of the design with fruit, chocolate or butterscotch sauce, or cream. Arrange the ice cream on top, keeping it within the border.

Spoon a little butterscotch or chocolate sauce over the base of a flat plate and tilt the plate to cover the bottom completely. Spoon melted white chocolate into a greaseproof paper bag, snip off the tip and pipe squiggly lines over the sauce. Leave to set, then arrange the ice cream.

sorbets, granitas & water ices

After a rich main course, nothing refreshes the palate better than a clean-tasting sorbet or water ice. Stock up the freezer when fruits are plentiful to make effortless desserts throughout the year. Slushy granitas are even easier, and introduce robust flavours such as coffee and ginger.

Lemon Sorbet

This is probably the most classic sorbet of all. Refreshingly tangy and yet deliciously smooth, it quite literally melts in the mouth.

SERVES SIX

INGREDIENTS

200g | 7oz | 1 cup CASTER SUGAR

300ml | ½ pint | 1¼ cups WATER

4 LEMONS, well scrubbed

1 EGG WHITE

SUGARED LEMON RIND, to decorate

1 Put the sugar and water into a saucepan and bring to the boil, stirring occasionally until the sugar has just dissolved.

2 Using a swivel vegetable peeler pare the rind thinly from two of the lemons so that it falls straight into the pan.

3 Simmer for 2 minutes without stirring, then take the pan off the heat. Leave to cool, then chill.

4 Squeeze the juice from all the lemons and add it to the syrup.

BY HAND: Strain the syrup into a shallow freezerproof container, reserving the rind. Freeze the mixture for 4 hours until it is mushy.

USING AN ICE CREAM MAKER: Strain the syrup and lemon juice and churn the mixture until thick.

5 BY HAND: Scoop the sorbet into a food processor and beat it until smooth. Lightly whisk the egg white with a fork until it is just frothy. Spoon the sorbet back into the tub, beat in the egg white and return the mixture to the freezer for 4 hours.

USING AN ICE CREAM MAKER: Add the egg white to the mixture and continue to churn for 10–15 minutes until firm enough to scoop.

6 Scoop into bowls or glasses and decorate with sugared lemon rind.

COOK'S TIP *Cut one third off the top of a lemon and retain as a lid. Squeeze the juice out of the larger portion. Remove any membrane and use the shell as a ready-made container. Scoop or pipe sorbet into the shell, top with lid and add lemon leaves or small bay leaves. Serve on a bed of crushed ice allowing one lemon per person.*

VARIATION *Sorbet can be made from any citrus fruit. As a guide you will need 300ml | ½ pint | 1¼ cups fresh fruit juice and the pared rind of half the squeezed fruits. Use 4 oranges or 2 oranges and 2 lemons, or, for a grapefruit sorbet, use the rind of one ruby grapefruit and the juice of two. For lime sorbet, combine the rind of three limes with the juice of six.*

Pear and Sauternes Sorbet

Based on a traditional sorbet that would have been served between savoury courses,

this fruity ice is delicately flavoured with the honied bouquet of

Sauternes wine, spiked with brandy.

SERVES SIX

INGREDIENTS

675g | 1½lb RIPE PEARS

50g | 2oz | ¼ cup CASTER SUGAR

250ml | 8fl oz | 1 cup WATER
plus 60ml | 4 tbsp extra

250ml | 8fl oz | 1 cup
SAUTERNES WINE,
plus extra to serve

30ml | 2 tbsp BRANDY

juice of ½ LEMON

1 EGG WHITE

FRESH MINT SPRIGS,
dusted with icing sugar,
to decorate

1 Quarter the pears, peel them and cut out the cores. Slice them into a saucepan and add the sugar and 60ml | 4 tbsp of the measured water. Cover and simmer for 10 minutes, or until the pears are just tender.

2 Tip the pear mixture into a food processor or blender and process until smooth, then scrape into a bowl. Leave to cool, then chill.

3 Stir the wine, brandy and lemon juice into the chilled pear purée with the remaining water.

4 BY HAND: Pour the mixture into a plastic tub or similar freezerproof container, freeze for 4 hours, then beat in a food processor or blender until smooth. Return the sorbet to the tub.

USING AN ICE CREAM MAKER:
Simply churn the pear mixture in an ice cream maker until thick.

5 Lightly whisk the egg white with a fork until just frothy. Either add to the sorbet in the ice cream maker, or stir into the sorbet in the tub. Churn or return to the freezer until the sorbet is firm enough to scoop. Serve the sorbet in small dessert glasses, with a little extra Sauternes poured over each portion. Decorate with the sugared mint sprigs.

COOK'S TIP *Sorbets that contain alcohol tend to take a long time to freeze, especially when made in an ice cream maker. To save time, transfer it to a tub as soon as it thickens and finish freezing it in the freezer. If you make the sorbet by hand, freeze the mixture in a stainless steel roasting tin to begin with. Transfer the sorbet to a plastic tub only after the egg white has been added.*

sorbets, granitas & water ices 63

Red Berry Sorbet

This vibrant red sorbet seems to capture the true flavour of summer. Pick your own berries, if you can, and use them as soon as possible.

SERVES SIX

INGREDIENTS

150g | 5oz | ¾ cup CASTER SUGAR

200ml | 7fl oz | scant 1 cup WATER

500g | 1¼lb | 5 cups
MIXED RIPE BERRIES, hulled,
including two or more
of the following:
STRAWBERRIES, RASPBERRIES,
TAYBERRIES or LOGANBERRIES

juice of ½ LEMON

1 EGG WHITE

small whole and halved
STRAWBERRIES and
STRAWBERRY LEAVES
and FLOWERS,
to decorate

1 Put the sugar and water into a saucepan and bring to the boil, stirring until the sugar has dissolved. Pour the syrup into a bowl, leave to cool, then chill.

2 Purée the fruits in a food processor or blender, then press through a sieve into a large bowl. Stir in the syrup and lemon juice.

3 BY HAND: Pour the mixture into a plastic tub or similar freezerproof container and freeze for 4 hours until mushy. Transfer to a food processor, process until smooth, then return to the tub. Lightly whisk the egg white and stir into the mixture. Freeze for 4 hours.

USING AN ICE CREAM MAKER: Churn until thick, then add the whisked egg white. Continue to churn until firm enough to scoop.

4 Scoop onto plates or bowls, and decorate with fresh strawberries, leaves and flowers.

VARIATION *For a fruity sorbet with a hidden kick, add 45ml | 3 tbsp vodka or cassis. Don't be too generous with the spirits or the sorbet will not freeze firm.*

Blackcurrant Sorbet

Wonderfully sharp and bursting with flavour, this is a very popular sorbet. If you find it a bit tart, add a little more sugar before freezing.

SERVES SIX

INGREDIENTS

500g | 1¼lb | 5 cups
BLACKCURRANTS, trimmed

350ml | 12fl oz | 1½ cups WATER

150g | 5oz | ¾ cup CASTER SUGAR

1 EGG WHITE

SPRIGS OF BLACKCURRANTS,
to decorate

1 Put the blackcurrants in a saucepan and add 150ml | ¼ pint | ⅔ cup of the measured water.

2 Cover the pan and simmer for 5 minutes or until the fruit is soft. Cool slightly, then purée in a food processor or blender.

3 Set a large sieve over a bowl, pour the purée into the sieve then press it through the mesh with the back of a spoon.

4 Pour the remaining measured water into the clean pan. Add the sugar and bring to the boil, stirring until the sugar has dissolved. Pour the syrup into a bowl. Cool, then chill. Mix the blackcurrant purée and sugar syrup together.

5 BY HAND: Spoon into a plastic tub or similar freezerproof container and freeze until mushy. Lightly whisk the egg white until just frothy. Spoon the sorbet into a food processor, process until smooth, then return it to the tub and stir in the egg white. Freeze for 4 hours or until firm.

USING AN ICE CREAM MAKER: Churn until thick. Add the egg white and continue churning until it is firm enough to scoop.

6 Serve decorated with the blackcurrant sprigs.

Strawberry and Lavender Sorbet

Delicately perfumed with just a hint of lavender,

this delightful pastel pink sorbet is perfect

for a special-occasion dinner.

SERVES SIX

INGREDIENTS

150g | 5oz | ¾ cup CASTER SUGAR

300ml | ½ pint | 1¼ cups WATER

6 FRESH LAVENDER FLOWERS

500g | 1¼lb | 5 cups
STRAWBERRIES, hulled

1 EGG WHITE

LAVENDER FLOWERS, to decorate

1 Bring the sugar and water to the boil in a saucepan, stirring until the sugar has dissolved.

2 Take the pan off the heat, add the lavender flowers and leave to infuse for 1 hour. If time permits, chill the syrup before using.

3 Purée the strawberries in a food processor or in batches in a blender, then press the purée through a large sieve into a bowl.

4 BY HAND: Pour the purée into a plastic tub, strain in the syrup and freeze for 4 hours until mushy. Transfer to a food processor and process until smooth. Whisk the egg white until frothy, and stir into the sorbet. Spoon the sorbet back into the tub and freeze until firm.

USING AN ICE CREAM MAKER: Pour the strawberry purée into the bowl and strain in the lavender syrup. Churn until thick. Add the whisked egg white to the ice cream maker and continue to churn until the sorbet is firm enough to scoop.

5 Serve in scoops, piled into tall glasses, and decorate with sprigs of lavender flowers.

COOK'S TIP *The size of the lavender flowers can vary; if they are very small you may need to use eight. To double check, taste a little of the cooled lavender syrup. If you think the flavour is a little mild, add 2–3 more flowers, reheat and cool again before using.*

Minted Earl Grey Sorbet

Originally favoured by the Georgians at grand summer balls, this refreshing, slightly tart sorbet is perfect for a lazy afternoon in the garden.

SERVES SIX

INGREDIENTS

200g | 7oz | 1 cup
CASTER SUGAR

300ml | ½ pint | 1¼ cups WATER

1 LEMON, well scrubbed

45ml | 3 tbsp EARL GREY
TEA LEAVES

450ml | ¾ pint | 2 cups
BOILING WATER

1 EGG WHITE

30ml | 2 tbsp chopped fresh MINT
LEAVES

FRESH MINT SPRIGS or
FROSTED MINT,
to decorate

1 Put the caster sugar and water into a saucepan and bring the mixture to the boil, stirring until the sugar has dissolved.

2 Thinly pare the rind from the lemon so that it falls straight into the pan of syrup. Simmer for 2 minutes then pour into a bowl. Cool, then chill.

3 Put the tea into a pan and pour on the boiling water. Cover and leave to stand for 5 minutes, then strain into a bowl. Cool, then chill.

4 BY HAND: Pour the tea into a plastic tub or similar freezerproof container. Strain in the chilled syrup. Freeze for 4 hours.

USING AN ICE CREAM MAKER: Combine the tea and syrup and churn the mixture until thick.

5 BY HAND: Lightly whisk the egg white until just frothy. Scoop the sorbet into a food processor, process until smooth and mix in the mint and egg white. Spoon back into the tub and freeze for 4 hours until firm.

USING AN ICE CREAM MAKER: Add the mint to the mixture. Lightly whisk the egg white until just frothy, then tip it into the ice cream maker and continue to churn until firm enough to scoop.

6 Serve in scoops, decorated with a few fresh or frosted mint leaves.

COOK'S TIP *If you only have Earl Grey tea bags these can be used instead, but add enough to make 450ml | ¾ pint | scant 2 cups strong tea. Make frosted mint leaves by dipping the leaves in egg white and sprinkling them with caster sugar.*

Coffee Granita

The most famous of all granitas, this originated in Mexico. It consists of full-bodied coffee frozen into tiny ice flakes.

SERVES SIX

INGREDIENTS

75ml | 5 tbsp good quality
GROUND FILTER COFFEE

1 litre | 1¾ pints | 4 cups
BOILING WATER

150g | 5oz | ¾ cup CASTER SUGAR

150ml | ¼ pint | ⅔ cup
DOUBLE CREAM (optional)

1 Spoon the coffee into a cafetière or jug, pour on the boiling water and leave to stand for 5 minutes. Plunge the cafetière or strain from the jug. Pour the coffee into a large plastic container, to a maximum depth of 2.5cm | 1in.

2 Add the sugar and stir until it has dissolved completely. Leave the mixture to cool.

3 Cover and freeze for 2 hours or until the coffee mixture around the sides of the container is starting to become mushy.

4 Using a fork, break up the ice crystals and mash the mixture finely. Return the granita to the freezer for 2 hours more, beating every 30 minutes until the ice becomes fine, even crystals.

5 After the final beating return the now slushy granita to the freezer. When ready to serve, spoon the granita into glass dishes. Whip the cream and offer it separately, if you like.

COOK'S TIP *If you taste the coffee before freezing, don't be alarmed by its strength; the change from liquid to ice mysteriously dulls the flavour, so the finished taste is just right.*

Raspberry Granita

This vibrant bright red granita looks spectacular. Served solo, it is an excellent dessert for anyone on a fat-free diet. For something a little more indulgent, serve with whole berries and creme fraiche or clotted cream, for an elegant and contemporary Knickerbocker Glory style dessert.

SERVES SIX

INGREDIENTS

115g | 4oz | ½ cup CASTER SUGAR

300ml | ½ pint | 1¼ cups WATER

500g | 1¼lb | 3½ cups RASPBERRIES, hulled, plus extra, to decorate

juice of 1 LEMON

little SIFTED ICING SUGAR, for dusting

1 Tip the sugar and water into a large saucepan and bring to the boil, stirring occasionally until the sugar has dissolved. Pour the sugar syrup into a bowl, leave to cool, then chill.

2 Purée the raspberries in a food processor or in batches in a blender. Spoon the purée into a fine sieve set over a large bowl. Press the purée through the sieve with the back of the spoon and then discard the seeds.

3 Scrape the purée into a large measuring jug, stir in the sugar syrup and lemon juice and top up to 1 litre | 1¾ pints | 4 cups with cold water.

4 Pour the mixture into a large plastic container so that the depth is no more than 2.5cm | 1in. Cover and freeze for 2 hours until the mixture around the sides of the container is mushy.

5 Using a fork, break up the ice crystals and mash finely. Return to the freezer for 2 hours, beating every 30 minutes until the ice forms fine, even crystals.

6 Spoon into tall glass dishes and decorate with extra raspberries dusted with a little sifted icing sugar, if you wish.

COOK'S TIP *For a granita with a little extra oomph, stir in 45ml | 3 tbsp cassis, but don't be tempted to add more or the granita will not freeze. If you miss one of the beatings, don't panic. Leave the granita at room temperature for 10–15 minutes to soften slightly, then beat thoroughly with a fork until it is the required consistency. Return it to the freezer and continue with the recipe.*

Watermelon Granita

*Pastel pink flakes of ice, subtly blended with the citrus freshness of
lime and the delicate flavour of watermelon, make this granita
a rare treat for the eye and the tastebuds.*

2 Discard most of the seeds, scoop
the flesh into a food processor and
process briefly until smooth.
Alternatively, use a blender, and
process the watermelon quarters in
small batches.

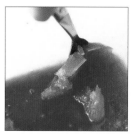

3 Strain the purée into a large
plastic container. Discard the
seeds. Pour in the chilled syrup,
lime rind and juice and mix well.

4 Cover and freeze for 2 hours
until the mixture around the sides
of the container is mushy. Mash
the ice finely with a fork and
return the granita to the freezer.

5 Freeze for 2 hours more,
mashing the mixture every
30 minutes, until the granita has
a fine slushy consistency. Scoop it
into dishes and serve with the
wedges of extra lime.

SERVES SIX

INGREDIENTS

150g | 5oz | ⅔ cup CASTER SUGAR

150ml | ¼ pint | ¾ cup WATER

1 whole WATERMELON,
about 1.75kg | 4–4½lb

FINELY GRATED RIND and
JUICE of 2 LIMES, plus LIME
WEDGES, for serving

1 Bring the sugar and water to the
boil in a saucepan, stirring until
the sugar has dissolved. Pour into a
bowl. Cool, then chill. Cut the
watermelon into quarters.

VARIATION *To serve this granita
cocktail-style, dip the rim of each glass
serving dish in a little water or beaten
egg white, then dip it into sugar. Spoon
in the granita, pour over a little
Cointreau, Tequila or white rum and
decorate with lime wedges or thin strips
of lime rind removed with a cannelle
knife and twisted around a cocktail stick.*

Tequila and Orange Granita

Full of flavour, this distinctive Mexican granita will have guests clamouring for more. Serve simply with wedges of citrus fruit or spoon over a little grenadine.

SERVES SIX

INGREDIENTS

115g | 4oz | ½ cup CASTER SUGAR

300ml | ½ pint | 1¼ cups WATER

6 ORANGES, well scrubbed

90ml | 6 tbsp TEQUILA

ORANGE and LIME WEDGES to decorate

1 Put the sugar and water into a saucepan. Using a vegetable peeler, thinly pare the rind from three of the oranges, letting it fall into the pan. Bring to the boil, stirring to dissolve the sugar. Pour the syrup into a bowl, cool, then chill.

2 Strain the syrup into a shallow plastic container. Squeeze all the oranges, strain the juice into the syrup then stir in the tequila. Check that the mixture is no more than 2.5cm | 1in deep; transfer to a larger container if needed.

3 Cover and freeze for 2 hours until the mixture around the sides of the container is mushy. Mash well with a fork and return the granita to the freezer.

4 Freeze for 2 hours more, mashing the mixture with a fork every 30 minutes until the granita has a fine slushy consistency. Scoop it into dishes and serve with the orange and lime wedges.

COOK'S TIP *If you don't have any tequila, make the granita with vodka, Cointreau, or even white rum. Don't be tempted to add more than the recommended amount; too much alcohol will stop the granita from freezing.*

Ruby Grapefruit Granita

This is slightly sharper than the other granitas, but is very refreshing. It's the ideal choice for serving after a rich or very filling main course.

SERVES SIX

INGREDIENTS

200g | 7oz | 1 cup CASTER SUGAR

300ml | ½ pint | 1¼ cups WATER

4 RUBY GRAPEFRUIT

TINY MINT LEAVES, to decorate

1 Put the sugar and water into a saucepan. Bring the water to the boil, stirring until the sugar has dissolved. Pour the syrup into a bowl, cool, then chill.

COOK'S TIP *Grapefruit shells make very good serving dishes. For a more modern treatment, consider the effect you would like to achieve when halving the grapefruit. They look great when tilted at an angle. Having squeezed the juice and removed the membrane, trim a little off the base of each shell so that it will remain stable when filled with granita.*

2 Cut the grapefruit in half. Squeeze the juice, taking care not to damage the grapefruit shells. Set these aside. Strain the juice into a large plastic container. Stir in the chilled syrup, making sure that the depth of the mixture does not exceed 2.5cm | 1in.

3 Cover and freeze for 2 hours or until the mixture around the sides of the container is mushy. Using a fork, break up the ice crystals and mash the granita finely.

4 Freeze for 2 hours more, mashing the mixture every 30 minutes until the granita consists of fine, even crystals.

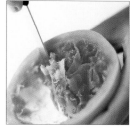

5 Select the six best grapefruit shells for use as the serving dishes. Using a sharp knife, remove the grapefruit pulp, leaving the shells as clean as possible.

6 Scoop the sorbet into the grapefruit shells, decorate with the tiny mint leaves and serve.

Ginger Granita

This full-bodied granita is a must for ginger lovers. Served solo, it is a simple and inexpensive dessert, yet is smart enough to serve to the most sophisticated guests.

SERVES SIX

INGREDIENTS

150g | 5oz | ¾ cup CASTER SUGAR

1 litre | 1¾ pints | 4 cups WATER

75g | 3oz ROOT GINGER

a little GROUND CINNAMON, to decorate

1 Put the sugar and water into a saucepan. Bring to the boil, stirring until the sugar has dissolved. Take the pan off the heat.

2 Peel the ginger, chop it finely, then stir it into the hot sugar syrup. Leave for at least 1 hour to infuse and cool, then pour into a bowl and chill.

3 Strain the chilled syrup into a large, shallow plastic container, making sure the depth is no more than 2.5cm | 1in. Cover and freeze for 2 hours or until the mixture around the sides of the container has become mushy.

4 Using a fork, break up the ice crystals and mash finely. Return the granita to the freezer for 2 hours more, beating every 30 minutes until the ice becomes soft and very fine with evenly sized ice crystals.

COOK'S TIP *You will be able to maintain the right texture for an hour or so but after that it will become too firm. To serve, spoon into tall glasses and dust with ground cinnamon.*

5 After the final beating, return the now slushy granita to the freezer. Serve in tall glasses decorated with ground cinnamon.

VARIATION *Whip 150ml | ¼ pint | ⅔ cup double cream and pipe it on top of each portion of granita. Decorate with crystallized ginger.*

Damson Water Ice

Use ripe fruits for natural sweetness. If you can't find damsons, use another deep-red variety of plum or extra-juicy Victoria plums.

SERVES SIX

INGREDIENTS

500g | 1¼lb RIPE DAMSONS, washed

450ml | ¾ pint | scant 2 cups WATER

150g | 5oz | ⅔ cup CASTER SUGAR

1 Put the damsons into a saucepan and add 150ml | ¼ pint | ⅔ cup of the water. Cover and simmer for 10 minutes or until the damsons are tender.

2 Pour the remaining water into a second saucepan. Add the sugar and bring to the boil, stirring until the sugar has dissolved. Pour the syrup into a bowl, leave to cool, then chill.

3 Break up the cooked damsons in the pan with a wooden spoon and scoop out any free stones. Pour the fruit and juices into a large sieve set over a bowl. Press the fruit through the sieve and discard the skins and any remaining stones from the sieve.

4 BY HAND: Pour the damson purée into a shallow plastic container. Stir in the syrup and freeze for 6 hours, beating once or twice to break up the ice crystals.

USING AN ICE CREAM MAKER: Mix the purée with the syrup and churn until firm enough to scoop.

5 Spoon into tall glasses or dishes and serve with wafer biscuits.

VARIATIONS *Apricot water ice can be made in the same way. Flavour the water ice with a little lemon or orange rind or add a broken cinnamon stick to the pan when poaching the fruit.*

Apple and Cider Water Ice

This very English combination has a subtle apple flavour with just a hint of cider. As the apple purée is very pale, almost white, add a few drops of green food colouring to echo the pale green skin of the Granny Smith apples.

SERVES SIX

INGREDIENTS

500g | 1¼lb GRANNY SMITH
APPLES

150g | 5oz | ¾ cup CASTER SUGAR

300ml | ½ pint | 1¼ cups WATER

250ml | 8fl oz | 1 cup
STRONG DRY CIDER

few drops of GREEN FOOD
COLOURING
(optional)

strips of thinly pared
LIME RIND, to decorate

1 Quarter, core and roughly chop the apples. Put them into a saucepan. Add the caster sugar and half the water. Cover and simmer for 10 minutes or until the apples are soft.

2 Press the mixture through a sieve placed over a bowl. Discard the apple skins and seeds. Stir the cider and the remaining water into the apple purée and add a little colouring, if you like.

3 BY HAND: Pour into a shallow plastic container and freeze for 6 hours, beating with a fork once or twice to break up the ice crystals.

USING AN ICE CREAM MAKER: Churn until firm enough to scoop.

4 Scoop into dishes and decorate with twists of thinly pared lime rind.

COOK'S TIP *Add the food colouring gradually, making the mixture a little darker than you would like the finished sorbet to be as freezing lightens the colour slightly.*

vanilla, chocolate & coffee ice creams

This chapter provides the best classic vanilla ice cream recipes plus some imaginative variations using ingredients such as brandied fruits, crumbled cookies, saffron, and cinnamon. The principal flavours of chocolate, coffee and toffee ice cream are many people's favourites, making this selection the ultimate collection of classic ice creams.

Classic Vanilla Ice Cream

Nothing beats the creamy simplicity of true vanilla ice cream. Vanilla pods are expensive, but well worth buying for the superb flavour they impart.

2 Lift the vanilla pod up. Holding it over the pan, scrape the black seeds out of the pod with a small knife so that they fall back into the milk. Set the vanilla pod aside and bring the milk back to the boil.

4 When the custard thickens and is smooth, pour it back into the bowl. Cool it, then chill.

SERVES FOUR

INGREDIENTS

1 VANILLA POD

300ml | ½ pint | 1¼ cups
SEMI-SKIMMED MILK

4 EGG YOLKS

75g | 3oz | 6 tbsp CASTER SUGAR

5ml | 1 tsp CORNFLOUR

300ml | ½ pint / 1¼ cups
DOUBLE CREAM

1 Using a small knife slit the vanilla pod lengthways. Pour the milk into a heavy-based saucepan, add the vanilla pod and bring to the boil. Remove from the heat and leave for 15 minutes to allow the flavours to infuse.

3 Whisk the egg yolks, sugar and cornflour in a bowl until the mixture is thick and foamy. Gradually pour on the hot milk, whisking constantly. Return the mixture to the pan and cook over a gentle heat, stirring all the time.

5 BY HAND: Whip the cream until it has thickened but still falls from a spoon. Fold it into the custard and pour into a plastic tub or similar freezerproof container. Freeze for 6 hours or until firm enough to scoop, beating twice with a fork, or in a food processor.

USING AN ICE CREAM MAKER: Stir the cream into the custard and churn the mixture until thick.

6 Scoop into dishes, bowls or bought cones – or eat straight from the tub.

COOK'S TIP *Don't throw the vanilla pod away after use. Instead, rinse it in cold water, dry and store in the sugar jar. After a week or so the sugar will take on the wonderful aroma and flavour of the vanilla and will be delicious sprinkled over summer fruits. Use it to sweeten whipped cream, custard, biscuits and shortbread.*

Brown Bread Ice Cream

This classic and very English ice cream is flecked with tiny clusters of crisp, crunchy caramelized brown breadcrumbs and tastes rather like the more modern American style cookies-and-cream ice cream.

SERVES FOUR TO SIX

INGREDIENTS

4 EGG YOLKS

75g | 3oz | 6 tbsp CASTER SUGAR

5ml | 1 tsp CORNFLOUR

300ml | ½ pint | 1¼ cups
SEMI-SKIMMED MILK

40g | 1½oz | 3 tbsp BUTTER

75g | 3oz | 1½ cups FRESH
BROWN BREADCRUMBS

50g | 2oz | ¼ cup
SOFT LIGHT BROWN SUGAR

5ml | 1 tsp NATURAL
VANILLA ESSENCE

300ml | ½ pint | 1¼ cups
DOUBLE CREAM

1 Whisk the egg yolks, sugar and cornflour together in a bowl until thick and pale. Pour the milk into a heavy-based saucepan, bring it just to the boil, then gradually pour it on to the egg yolk mixture, whisking constantly.

2 Return the mixture to the pan and cook over a gentle heat, stirring constantly until the custard thickens and is smooth. Pour it back into the bowl, leave to cool, then chill.

COOK'S TIP *Watch the breadcrumbs carefully when frying. Like almonds, they have a habit of burning if you turn your back on them for a moment, and burnt crumbs will give the ice cream a bitter taste. The crumbs should darken only slightly.*

3 Melt the butter in a large frying pan. Add the breadcrumbs, stir until evenly coated in butter, then sprinkle the sugar over. Fry gently for 4–5 minutes, stirring until lightly browned. Remove from the heat and leave until cool and crisp.

4 BY HAND: Add the vanilla essence to the custard and mix well. Whip the cream until thick then fold into the custard. Pour into a plastic tub or similar freezerproof container. Freeze for 4 hours, beating once with a fork to break up the crystals.

USING AN ICE CREAM MAKER: Add the vanilla essence to the custard and mix well. Stir in the cream. Transfer to the ice cream maker and churn until thick.

5 BY HAND: Break up the breadcrumbs with your fingers. Beat the ice cream briefly, then stir in the breadcrumbs. Return the tub to the freezer and leave until firm enough to scoop.

USING AN ICE CREAM MAKER: Rub the breadcrumbs between your fingers to break up any lumps. Stir the breadcrumbs into the mixture, churn for 5–10 minutes until ready

Crème Fraîche and Honey Ice

This delicately flavoured vanilla ice cream is delicious either served on its own or with slices of hot apple or cherry pie.

SERVES FOUR

INGREDIENTS

4 EGG YOLKS

60ml | 4 tbsp CLEAR FLOWER HONEY

5ml | 1 tsp CORNFLOUR

300ml | ½ pint | 1¼ cups SEMI-SKIMMED MILK

7.5ml | 1½ tsp NATURAL VANILLA ESSENCE

250g | 9oz | generous 1 cup CRÈME FRAÎCHE

NASTURTIUM, PANSY or HERB FLOWERS, to decorate

1 Whisk the egg yolks, honey and cornflour in a bowl until thick and foamy. Pour the milk into a heavy-based saucepan, bring to the boil, then gradually pour on to the yolk mixture, whisking constantly.

2 Return the mixture to the pan and cook over a gentle heat, stirring all the time until the custard thickens and is smooth. Pour it back into the bowl, then chill.

3 BY HAND: Stir in the vanilla essence and crème fraîche. Pour into a plastic tub or similar freezerproof container. Freeze for 6 hours or until firm enough to scoop, beating once or twice with a fork or in a food processor to break up the ice crystals.

USING AN ICE CREAM MAKER: Stir the vanilla essence and crème fraîche into the custard mix and churn until thick and firm enough to scoop.

4 Serve in glass dishes and decorate with nasturtiums, pansies or herb flowers.

COOK'S TIP *Measure the honey carefully and use level spoonfuls; if you are over-generous, the honey flavour will dominate and the ice cream will be too sweet.*

Tutti Frutti

This Italian fruit ice cream takes its name from an expression meaning "all the fruits".

Four fruits have been used here but you can make up your own blend of candied

or glacé fruits, including exotics such as papaya or mango.

SERVES FOUR TO SIX

INGREDIENTS

300ml | ½ pint | 1¼ cups
SEMI-SKIMMED MILK

1 VANILLA POD

4 EGG YOLKS

75g | 3oz | 6 tbsp CASTER SUGAR

5ml | 1 tsp CORNFLOUR

300ml | ½ pint | 1¼ cups
WHIPPING CREAM

150g | 5oz | ⅔ cup
MULTI-COLOURED
GLACÉ CHERRIES

50g | 2oz | ⅓ cup
SLICED CANDIED LIME and
ORANGE PEEL

50g | 2oz | ⅓ cup
CANDIED PINEAPPLE

1 Pour the milk into a heavy-based saucepan. Using a small, sharp knife slit the vanilla pod lengthways, add it to the milk and bring to the boil. Immediately remove the pan from the heat and leave the milk for 15 minutes to allow the flavour to infuse.

2 Lift up the vanilla pod. Holding it over the pan of milk, scrape out the small black seeds with a narrow-bladed knife so that they fall into the milk. Set the vanilla pod aside, for later re-use, and bring the flavoured milk back to the boil over a gentle heat.

3 Meanwhile, whisk the egg yolks, sugar and cornflour in a bowl until thick and foamy. Gradually whisk in the flavoured milk.

4 Pour the milk mixture back into the pan. Cook over a gentle heat, stirring constantly until the custard thickens. Pour it back into the bowl and cover. Cool, then chill.

5 BY HAND: Whip the cream until it has thickened but is still soft enough to fall from a spoon, then fold it into the custard.

USING AN ICE CREAM MAKER: Mix the thickened custard with the cream. There is no need to whip the cream first. Churn the custard and cream mixture until it is thick.

6 BY HAND: Pour the mixture into a plastic tub or similar freezerproof container. Freeze for 4 hours, beating once with a fork or electric mixer to break up the ice crystals. If you prefer, break up the crystals by blending the mixture briefly in a food processor.

7 Finely chop the glacé cherries, candied peel and pineapple and fold into the ice cream. Return to the freezer for 2–3 hours or churn in the ice cream maker for 5–10 minutes until firm enough to scoop.

VARIATION *Steep the glacé fruits in a little Kirsch for 3 hours before adding.*

Cookies and Cream

This wickedly indulgent ice cream is a favourite in the USA. To make the result even more luxurious, use
freshly baked home-made biscuits with large chunks of chocolate and nuts.

SERVES FOUR TO SIX

INGREDIENTS

4 EGG YOLKS

75g | 3oz | 6 tbsp CASTER SUGAR

5ml | 1 tsp CORNFLOUR

300ml | ½ pint | 1¼ cups
SEMI-SKIMMED MILK

5ml | 1 tsp NATURAL VANILLA
ESSENCE

300ml | ½ pint | 1¼ cups
WHIPPING CREAM

150g | 5oz CHUNKY CHOCOLATE
AND HAZELNUT BISCUITS,
crumbled into chunky pieces

1 Whisk the egg yolks, sugar and cornflour in a bowl until the mixture is thick and foamy. Pour the milk into a heavy-based saucepan, bring it just to the boil, then pour it on to the yolk mixture, whisking constantly.

2 Return to the pan and cook over a gentle heat, stirring until the custard thickens and is smooth. Pour it back into the bowl and cover closely. Leave to cool, then chill.

3 BY HAND: Stir the vanilla essence into the custard. Whip the cream until it is thickened but is still soft enough to fall from a spoon.

USING AN ICE CREAM MAKER: Stir the vanilla essence into the custard. Stir in the whipping cream and churn until thick.

4 BY HAND: Fold the cream into the chilled custard, then pour into a plastic tub or similar freezerproof container. Freeze for 4 hours, beating once with a fork, electric whisk or in a food processor to break up the ice crystals. Beat one more time, then fold in the biscuit chunks. Cover and return to the freezer until firm.

USING AN ICE CREAM MAKER: Churn until thick enough to scoop then scrape the ice cream into a freezerproof container. Fold in the biscuit chunks and freeze for 2–3 hours until firm.

COOK'S TIP *Experiment with different types of biscuit to find the type that gives the best results.*

Brandied Fruit and Rice Ice Cream

Based on a favourite Victorian rice ice cream, this rich dessert combines spicy rice pudding with a creamy egg custard flecked with brandy-soaked fruits. The mixture is then frozen until it is just firm enough to scoop.

SERVES FOUR TO SIX

INGREDIENTS

50g | 2oz | ⅓ cup
READY-TO-EAT
STONED PRUNES

50g | 2oz | ⅓ cup
READY-TO-EAT
DRIED APRICOTS

50g | 2oz | ¼ cup
GLACÉ CHERRIES

30ml | 2 tbsp BRANDY

150ml | ¼ pint | ⅔ cup
SINGLE CREAM

For the rice mixture

40g | 1½oz | generous ¼ cup
PUDDING RICE

450ml | ¾ pint | scant 2 cups
FULL-CREAM MILK

1 CINNAMON STICK,
halved, plus extra CINNAMON
STICKS, to decorate

4 CLOVES

For the custard

4 EGG YOLKS

75g | 3oz | 6 tbsp CASTER SUGAR

5ml | 1 tsp CORNFLOUR

300ml | ½ pint | 1¼ cups
FULL-CREAM MILK

1 Chop the prunes, apricots and glacé cherries finely and put them in a bowl. Pour over the brandy. Cover and leave to soak for 3 hours or overnight if possible.

2 Put the rice, milk and whole spices in a saucepan. Bring to the boil, then simmer gently for 30 minutes, stirring occasionally until most of the milk has been absorbed. Lift out the spices and leave the rice to cool.

3 Whisk the egg yolks, sugar and cornflour in a bowl until thick and foamy. Heat the milk in a heavy-based pan then gradually pour it on to the yolks, whisking constantly. Pour back into the pan and cook, stirring until the custard thickens. Leave to cool, then chill.

4 BY HAND: Mix the chilled custard, rice and cream together. Pour into a plastic tub or similar freezerproof container and freeze for 4–5 hours until mushy then beat the ice cream lightly with a fork to break up the ice crystals.

USING AN ICE CREAM MAKER: Mix the chilled custard, rice and cream together. Churn until thick.

5 BY HAND: Fold in the fruits then freeze for 2–3 hours until firm enough to scoop.

USING AN ICE CREAM MAKER: Spoon the ice cream into a freezerproof container and fold in the fruits. Freeze for 2–3 hours until firm.

6 Serve the ice cream in scoops decorated with cinnamon sticks.

COOK'S TIP *As the brandy-soaked fruits are so soft, it is better to remove the ice cream from the ice cream maker, fold in the fruits and then freeze the mixture in a tub until firm enough to scoop. This way, the fruits do not disintegrate and their colours are preserved. If you make the ice cream by hand, do not process it to break up ice crystals or the texture of the rice will be lost.*

Classic Dark Chocolate

Rich, dark and wonderfully luxurious, this ice cream can be served solo or drizzled with warm chocolate sauce.
If you are making it in advance, don't forget to soften the ice cream before serving so that the
full flavour of the chocolate comes through.

SERVES FOUR TO SIX

INGREDIENTS

4 EGG YOLKS

75g | 3oz | 6 tbsp CASTER SUGAR

5ml | 1 tsp CORNFLOUR

300ml | ½ pint | 1¼ cups
SEMI-SKIMMED MILK

200g | 7oz DARK CHOCOLATE

300ml | ½ pint | 1¼ cups
WHIPPING CREAM

SHAVED CHOCOLATE,
to decorate

1 Whisk the egg yolks, sugar and cornflour in a bowl until thick and foamy. Pour the milk into a saucepan, bring it just to the boil, then gradually whisk it into the yolk mixture.

2 Return the mixture to the pan and cook over a gentle heat, stirring constantly until the custard thickens and is smooth. Take the pan off the heat.

3 Break the chocolate into small pieces and stir into the hot custard until it has melted. Leave to cool, then chill.

4 BY HAND: Whip the cream until it has thickened but still falls from a spoon. Fold into the custard then pour into a plastic tub or similar freezerproof container. Freeze for 6 hours or until firm enough to scoop, beating once or twice with a fork or in a food processor.

USING AN ICE CREAM MAKER: Mix the chocolate custard with the whipping cream. Churn until firm enough to scoop.

5 Serve in scoops, decorated with chocolate shavings.

COOK'S TIP *For the best flavour use a good quality chocolate with at least 75% cocoa solids, such as top-of-the-range Belgian dark chocolate or Continental-style dark cooking chocolate.*

Chocolate Double Mint

Full of body and flavour, this creamy, smooth ice cream combines the sophistication of dark chocolate with the satisfying coolness of fresh chopped mint. Crushed peppermints provide extra crunch.

SERVES FOUR

INGREDIENTS

4 EGG YOLKS

75g | 3oz | 6 tbsp CASTER SUGAR

5ml | 1 tsp CORNFLOUR

300ml | ½ pint | 1¼ cups
SEMI-SKIMMED MILK

200g | 7oz DARK CHOCOLATE,
broken into squares

40g | 1½oz | ¼ cup PEPPERMINTS

60ml | 4 tbsp CHOPPED
FRESH MINT

300ml | ½ pint | 1¼ cups
WHIPPING CREAM

sprigs of FRESH MINT dusted with
ICING SUGAR, to decorate

1 Put the egg yolks, sugar and cornflour in a bowl and whisk until thick and foamy. Pour the milk into a heavy-based saucepan, bring to the boil, then gradually whisk into the yolk mixture.

2 Scrape the mixture back into the pan and cook over a gentle heat, stirring constantly until the custard thickens and is smooth. Scrape it back into the bowl, add the chocolate, a little at a time, and stir until melted. Cool, then chill.

3 Put the peppermints in a strong plastic bag and crush them with a rolling pin. Stir them into the custard with the chopped mint.

4 BY HAND: Whip the cream until it has thickened, but is still soft enough to fall from a spoon. Fold it into the custard, scrape the mixture into a plastic tub or similar freezerproof container and freeze for 6–7 hours, beating once or twice with a fork or electric whisk to break up the ice crystals.

USING AN ICE CREAM MAKER: Mix the custard and cream together and churn the mixture until firm enough to scoop.

5 Serve the ice cream in scoops and then decorate with mint sprigs dusted with sifted icing sugar.

COOK'S TIP *If you freeze the ice cream in a tub, don't beat it in a food processor when breaking up the ice crystals or the crunchy texture of the crushed peppermints will be lost.*

Dark Chocolate and Hazelnut Praline Ice Cream

For nut lovers and chocoholics everywhere, this luxurious combination is the ultimate indulgence. For a change, you might like to try using other types of nuts for the praline instead.

SERVES FOUR TO SIX

INGREDIENTS

4 EGG YOLKS

5ml | 1 tsp CORNFLOUR

175g | 6oz | scant 1 cup
GRANULATED SUGAR

300ml | ½ pint | 1¼ cups
SEMI-SKIMMED MILK

150g | 5oz DARK CHOCOLATE,
broken into squares

115g | 4oz | 1 cup HAZELNUTS

60ml | 4 tbsp WATER

300ml | ½ pint | 1¼ cups
WHIPPING CREAM

1 Put the egg yolks in a bowl and add the cornflour, with half the sugar. Whisk until thick and foamy. Bring the milk just to the boil in a heavy-based saucepan then gradually pour it on to the yolk mixture, whisking constantly. Scrape back into the pan and cook over a gentle heat, stirring constantly, until the custard has thickened and is smooth.

2 Take the pan off the heat and stir the chocolate into the hot custard, a few squares at a time. Cool, then chill. Brush a baking sheet with oil and set it aside.

3 Meanwhile put the hazelnuts, remaining sugar and measured water in a large, heavy-based frying pan. Place over a gentle heat and heat without stirring until the sugar has dissolved.

4 Increase the heat slightly and cook until the syrup surrounding the nuts has turned pale golden. Quickly pour the mixture on to the oiled baking sheet and leave until the praline cools and hardens.

5 BY HAND: Whip the cream until it has thickened but still soft enough to fall from a spoon. Fold it into the custard and pour the mixture into a freezerproof container. Freeze for 4 hours, beating once with a fork or in a food processor to break up the ice crystals.

USING AN ICE CREAM MAKER: Pour the chocolate custard into the ice cream maker and add the cream. Churn for 25 minutes until thick and firm enough to scoop.

6 Break the praline into pieces. Reserve a few pieces for decoration and finely chop the rest.

7 BY HAND: Beat it once more, then fold in the chopped praline. Freeze for 2–3 hours or until firm.

USING AN ICE CREAM MAKER: Scrape the ice cream into a tub and stir in the praline. Freeze for 2–3 hours or until firm enough to scoop.

8 Scoop on to plates and decorate with the reserved praline.

Triple Chocolate Terrine

This variation on the popular Neapolitan layered ice cream is made with smooth, dark, milk and white chocolate. Serve it in slices, sandwiched between rectangular wafer biscuits or in a pool of warm dark chocolate sauce.

SERVES EIGHT TO TEN

INGREDIENTS

6 EGG YOLKS

115g | 4oz | ½ cup CASTER SUGAR

5ml | 1 tsp CORNFLOUR

450ml | ¾ pint | scant 2 cups
SEMI-SKIMMED MILK

115g | 4oz DARK CHOCOLATE,
broken into squares

115g | 4oz MILK CHOCOLATE,
broken into squares

115g | 4oz WHITE CHOCOLATE,
broken into squares

2.5ml | ½ tsp
NATURAL VANILLA ESSENCE

450ml | ¾ pint | scant 2 cups
WHIPPING CREAM

1 Whisk the egg yolks, sugar and cornflour in a bowl until thick and foamy. Pour the milk into a heavy-based saucepan and bring it to the boil. Gradually pour it on to the yolk mixture, whisking constantly, then return the mixture to the pan and cook over a gentle heat, stirring constantly until the custard thickens and is smooth.

2 Divide the custard equally among three bowls of equal size. Add the dark chocolate to one bowl, the milk chocolate to another and the white chocolate and vanilla essence to the third.

3 Stir with separate spoons until the chocolate has melted. Cool, then chill. Line a 25 x 7.5 x 7.5cm | 10 x 3 x 3in terrine or large loaf tin with clear film.

4 BY HAND: Whip the cream until it has just thickened but still falls from a spoon, divide among the bowls and fold into the custard. Pour each flavour into a separate tub or similar freezerproof container and freeze for 3–4 hours until thickened. Beat with a fork or electric mixer until smooth.

USING AN ICE CREAM MAKER: Stir a third of the cream into each bowl, then churn the milk chocolate custard mixture until thick. Return the remaining bowls of flavoured custard and cream to the fridge.

5 BY HAND: Spoon the milk chocolate ice cream into the lined tin, level the surface using the back of a spoon and freeze until firm. Spoon the white chocolate ice cream into the tin, level the surface and freeze until firm. Repeat the process with the dark chocolate ice cream, making sure the surface is smooth and level.

USING AN ICE CREAM MAKER: Churn the white chocolate ice cream until thick and smooth then spoon it into the tin. Level the surface and freeze until firm. Continue in the same way with the white chocolate and, finally, with the dark chocolate

6 Cover the terrine with clear film, then freeze it overnight. To serve, remove the clear film cover, then invert on to a plate. Peel off the clear film and serve in slices.

COOK'S TIP *Make sure each layer of ice cream is firm before adding another or the layers may merge. If you have made the ice cream by hand, the dark chocolate layer may need to be softened at room temperature before spreading.*

Chunky Chocolate Ice Cream

The three different chocolates in this decadent ice cream make it so delectable that it will rapidly disappear unless you hide it at the back of the freezer.

SERVES FOUR TO SIX

INGREDIENTS

4 EGG YOLKS

75g | 3oz | 6 tbsp CASTER SUGAR

5ml | 1 tsp CORNFLOUR

300ml | ½ pint | 1¼ cups
SEMI-SKIMMED MILK

200g | 7oz MILK CHOCOLATE

50g | 2oz DARK CHOCOLATE,
plus extra, to decorate

50g | 2oz WHITE CHOCOLATE

300ml | ½ pint | 1¼ cups
WHIPPING CREAM

1 Whisk the egg yolks, caster sugar and cornflour in a bowl until the mixture is thick and foamy. Pour the milk into a large, heavy-based saucepan. Heat the milk and bring it just to the boil, then gradually pour it on to the egg yolk mixture, whisking constantly.

2 Return the custard mixture to the pan and cook over a gentle heat, stirring constantly with a wooden spoon until the custard thickens and is smooth.

3 Pour the custard back into the bowl. Break 150g | 5oz of the milk chocolate into squares, stir these into the hot custard, then cover closely. Leave to cool, then chill. Chop the remaining milk, dark and white chocolate finely and reserve to use as decoration.

4 BY HAND: Whip the cream until it has thickened but is still soft enough to fall from a spoon.

USING AN ICE CREAM MAKER: Mix the chocolate custard and the whipping cream and churn for 25–30 minutes until thick.

5 BY HAND: Fold the whipped cream into the custard, pour into a plastic tub or similar freezerproof container and freeze for 4 hours, beating once with a fork, electric whisk or in a food processor.

USING AN ICE CREAM MAKER: Scoop the churned ice cream out of the machine and into a plastic tub.

6 BY HAND: Beat the ice cream one more time. Fold in the pieces of chocolate and freeze for at least 2–3 hours, or until firm enough to scoop. Decorate with more pieces of chocolate.

USING AN ICE CREAM MAKER: Fold in the pieces of chocolate and freeze for 2–3 hours until firm enough to scoop. Decorate with more pieces of chocolate.

COOK'S TIP *For maximum flavour, use good quality Belgian chocolate or your favourite chocolate bar; avoid using dark, milk or white cake covering.*

Chocolate Ripple Ice Cream

SERVES FOUR TO SIX

INGREDIENTS

4 EGG YOLKS

75g | 3oz | 6 tbsp CASTER SUGAR

5ml | 1 tsp CORNFLOUR

300ml | ½ pint | 1¼ cups
SEMI-SKIMMED MILK

250g | 9oz DARK CHOCOLATE,
broken into squares

25g | 1oz | 2 tbsp BUTTER, diced

30ml | 2 tbsp GOLDEN SYRUP

90ml | 6 tbsp SINGLE CREAM or
CREAM and MILK MIXED

300ml | ½ pint | 1¼ cups
WHIPPING CREAM

WAFER BISCUITS,
to serve

This creamy, dark chocolate ice cream, unevenly rippled with wonderful swirls of rich chocolate sauce, will stay deliciously soft even after freezing. Not that it will remain in the freezer for long!

1 Put the egg yolks, sugar and cornflour in a bowl and whisk until thick and foamy. Pour the milk into a heavy-based saucepan, bring it just to the boil, then gradually pour it on to the yolk mixture, whisking constantly.

2 Return the mixture to the pan and cook over a gentle heat, stirring constantly until the custard thickens and is smooth. Pour it back into the bowl and stir in 150g | 5oz of the chocolate until melted. Cover the chocolate custard closely, leave it to cool, then chill.

3 Put the remaining chocolate into a saucepan and add the butter. Spoon in the golden syrup. Heat gently, stirring, until the chocolate and butter have melted.

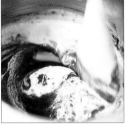

4 Stir in the single cream or cream and milk mixture. Heat gently, stirring, until smooth then leave the chocolate sauce to cool.

5 BY HAND: Whip the cream until it has thickened, but is still soft enough to fall from a spoon. Fold it into the custard, pour into a plastic tub or similar freezerproof container and freeze for 5 hours until thick, beating once with a fork or electric whisk or in a food processor. Beat the ice cream in the tub one more time.

USING AN ICE CREAM MAKER: Stir the cream into the custard and churn the mixture for 20–25 minutes until thick.

6 Add alternate spoonfuls of ice cream and chocolate sauce to a 1.5 litre | 2½ pint | 6 cup plastic container. Freeze for 5–6 hours until firm. Serve with wafers.

Chocolate and Brandy Parfait

This parfait is traditionally made with a mixture of chocolate and coffee, but here it is blended with cocoa powder for extra strength. Melted Belgian chocolate and a generous tot of brandy are the secret of its superb flavour.

SERVES SIX

INGREDIENTS

45ml | 3 tbsp COCOA POWDER

60ml | 4 tbsp BOILING WATER

150g | 5oz DARK CHOCOLATE, broken into squares

4 EGG YOLKS

115g | 4oz | ½ cup CASTER SUGAR

120ml | 4fl oz | ½ cup WATER

300ml | ½ pint | 1¼ cups DOUBLE CREAM

60–75ml | 4–5 tbsp BRANDY

drizzled WHITE CHOCOLATE RINGS, to decorate

1 Mix the cocoa to a paste with the boiling water. Put the chocolate into a heatproof bowl. Bring a pan of water to the boil, remove from the heat and place the bowl on top until the chocolate melts. In a separate bowl, whisk the yolks until frothy.

2 Heat the sugar and measured water gently in a saucepan, stirring occasionally, until dissolved, then boil for 4–5 minutes, without stirring, until it registers 115°C | 239°F on a sugar thermometer. You can also test by dropping a little syrup into cold water. The syrup should make a soft ball.

3 Quickly whisk the syrup into the yolks. Lift the bowl of chocolate off the pan and bring the water to a simmer. Place the bowl with the yolk mixture on top and whisk until very thick. Lift it off the pan and continue whisking until cool.

4 Whisk in the cocoa mixture, then fold in the melted chocolate. Whip the cream lightly and fold it in, with the brandy. Pour the mixture into 6–8 freezerproof serving dishes, then freeze for 4 hours or until firm. Decorate with white chocolate rings, made by drizzling melted white chocolate on non-stick baking parchment and leaving it to set.

COOK'S TIP *If you are not sure whether the syrup is ready it is better to use it sooner rather than later. If it is overboiled it will set like a rock when added to the cool yolks.*

Double White Chocolate Ice Cream

Crunchy chunks of white chocolate are a bonus in this delicious ice cream. Serve it scooped in waffle cones dipped in dark chocolate, for a sensational treat.

SERVES EIGHT

INGREDIENTS

4 EGG YOLKS

75g | 3oz | 6 tbsp CASTER SUGAR

5ml | 1 tsp CORNFLOUR

300ml | ½ pint | 1¼ cups SEMI-SKIMMED MILK

250g | 9oz WHITE CHOCOLATE, chopped

10ml | 2 tsp NATURAL VANILLA ESSENCE

300ml | ½ pint | 1¼ cups WHIPPING CREAM

8 CHOCOLATE DIPPED CONES, to serve

1 Whisk the egg yolks, sugar and cornflour in a bowl until the mixture is thick and foamy. Pour the milk into a heavy-based saucepan, bring it to the boil, then gradually pour it on to the yolk mixture, whisking constantly.

2 Return the custard mixture to the saucepan and cook over a gentle heat, stirring constantly until the custard thickens and is smooth. Pour the hot custard back into the same bowl.

3 Add 150g | 5oz of the chopped white chocolate to the hot custard, with the vanilla essence. Gently stir until the chocolate has melted, leave to cool, then chill.

4 **BY HAND:** Whip the cream until it has thickened but still falls from a spoon. Fold it into the custard and pour into a plastic tub or similar freezerproof container. Freeze for 4 hours, beating once with a fork or electric whisk or in a food processor. Beat the ice cream again, then stir in the remaining chocolate and return to the freezer for 2 hours.

USING AN ICE CREAM MAKER: Stir the cream into the custard, then churn the mixture until thick. Add the remaining chocolate and churn for 5–10 minutes until firm. Serve in chocolate dipped cones.

VARIATION *If you prefer, scoop the ice cream into glass dishes and decorate with white chocolate curls or extra diced chocolate. Ice cream served this way won't go quite as far, so will only serve 4–6.*

C 'n' C Sherbet

This dark chocolate sherbet is a cross between a water ice and a light cream-free ice cream, and is ideal for chocoholics who are trying to count calories.

SERVES FOUR TO SIX

INGREDIENTS

600ml | 1 pint | 2½ cups
SEMI-SKIMMED MILK

40g | 1½oz | ⅓ cup GOOD QUALITY
COCOA POWDER
(such as VAN HOUTEN)

115g | 4oz | ½ cup CASTER SUGAR

5ml | 1 tsp INSTANT COFFEE
GRANULES

CHOCOLATE-COVERED RAISINS,
to decorate

1 Heat the milk in a saucepan. Meanwhile, put the cocoa in a bowl. Add a little of the hot milk to the cocoa and mix to a paste.

2 Add the remaining milk to the cocoa mixture, stirring all the time, then pour the chocolate milk back into the saucepan. Bring to the boil, stirring continuously.

3 Take the pan off the heat and stir in the sugar and the coffee granules. Pour into a jug, leave to cool, then chill well.

4 BY HAND: Pour the mixture into a plastic tub or similar freezerproof container and freeze for 6 hours until firm, beating once or twice with a fork, electric mixer or in a food processor to break up the ice crystals. Allow to soften slightly before scooping into dishes. Sprinkle each portion with a few chocolate-covered raisins.

ICE CREAM MAKER: Churn the chilled mixture until very thick. Scoop into dishes. Sprinkle each portion with a few chocolate-covered raisins.

COOK'S TIP *Use good quality cocoa and don't overheat the milk mixture or the finished ice may taste bitter. If there are any lumps of cocoa in the milk, beat the mixture with a balloon whisk to remove them.*

Iced Tiramisu

This favourite Italian combination is not usually served as a frozen dessert, but it does make a marvellous ice cream. Like the more traditional version, it tastes very rich, despite the fact that virtually fat-free fromage frais is a major ingredient.

SERVES FOUR

INGREDIENTS

150g | 5oz | ¾ cup CASTER SUGAR

150ml | ¼ pint | ⅔ cup WATER

250g | 9oz | generous 1 cup MASCARPONE

200g | 7oz | scant 1 cup VIRTUALLY FAT-FREE FROMAGE FRAIS

5ml | 1 tsp NATURAL VANILLA ESSENCE

10ml | 2 tsp INSTANT COFFEE, dissolved in 30ml | 2 tbsp BOILING WATER

30ml | 2 tbsp COFFEE LIQUEUR or BRANDY

75g | 3oz SPONGE FINGER BISCUITS

COCOA POWDER, for dusting

CHOCOLATE CURLS, to decorate

1 Put 115g | 4oz | ½ cup of the sugar into a small saucepan. Add the water and bring to the boil, stirring until the sugar has dissolved. Leave the syrup to cool, then chill it.

2 Put the mascarpone into a bowl. Beat it with a spoon until it is soft, then stir in the fromage frais. Add the chilled sugar syrup, a little at a time, then stir in the vanilla essence.

3 BY HAND: Spoon the mixture into a plastic tub or similar freezerproof container and freeze for 4 hours, beating once with a fork, electric mixer or in a food processor to break up the ice crystals.

USING AN ICE CREAM MAKER: Churn the mascarpone mixture until it is thick but too soft to scoop.

4 Meanwhile, put the instant coffee mixture in a small bowl, sweeten with the remaining sugar, then add the liqueur or brandy. Stir well and leave to cool.

5 Crumble the biscuits into small pieces and toss them in the coffee mixture. If you have made the ice cream by hand, beat it again.

6 Spoon a third of the ice cream into a 900ml | 1½ pint | 3¾ cup plastic container, spoon over half the biscuits then top with half the remaining ice cream.

7 Sprinkle over the last of the coffee-soaked biscuits, then cover with the remaining ice cream. Freeze for 2–3 hours until firm enough to scoop. Dust with cocoa powder and spoon into glass dishes. Decorate with chocolate curls, and serve.

Classic Coffee Ice Cream

This bittersweet blend is a must for those who like their coffee strong and dark with just a hint of cream. When serving, decorate with the chocolate-covered coffee beans that are available from some larger supermarkets and high-class confectioners.

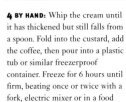

4 BY HAND: Whip the cream until it has thickened but still falls from a spoon. Fold into the custard, add the coffee, then pour into a plastic tub or similar freezerproof container. Freeze for 6 hours until firm, beating once or twice with a fork, electric mixer or in a food processor to break up the crystals.

ICE CREAM MAKER: Mix the coffee and cream with the chilled custard, then churn the mixture until firm enough to scoop.

5 Scoop the ice cream into glass dishes, sprinkle with chocolate-covered coffee beans and serve.

SERVES FOUR TO SIX

INGREDIENTS

90ml | 6 tbsp FINE FILTER COFFEE

250ml | 8fl oz | 1 cup
BOILING WATER

4 EGG YOLKS

75g | 3oz | 6 tbsp CASTER SUGAR

5ml | 1 tsp CORNFLOUR

300ml | ½ pint | 1¼ cups
SEMI-SKIMMED MILK

150ml | ¼ pint | ⅔ cup
DOUBLE CREAM

CHOCOLATE-COVERED
COFFEE BEANS, to decorate

1 Put the coffee in a cafetière or jug and pour on the boiling water. Leave to cool, then strain and chill until required.

2 Whisk the egg yolks, caster sugar and cornflour in a bowl until the mixture is thick and foamy. Pour the milk into a heavy-based saucepan, bring to the boil, then gradually pour on to the yolk mixture, whisking constantly.

3 Return the mixture to the pan and cook over a gentle heat, stirring all the time until the custard thickens and is smooth. Pour it back into the bowl and cover closely with clear film. Cool, then chill.

COOK'S TIP *If you only have coffee beans, put 50g | 2oz | ¼ cup in a mortar and crush with a pestle. Bring 300ml | ½ pint | 1¼ cups semi-skimmed milk to the boil, and infuse crushed beans for 15 minutes. Strain and use the flavoured milk to make the custard.*

Coffee Toffee Swirl

A wonderful combination of creamy vanilla, marbled with coffee flavoured toffee. Serve on its own or as a sundae with classic coffee and chocolate ice cream.

SERVES FOUR TO SIX

INGREDIENTS

For the toffee sauce

10ml/2 tsp CORNFLOUR

170g | 5¾oz can
EVAPORATED MILK

75g | 3oz | 6 tbsp
MUSCOVADO SUGAR

20ml | 4 tsp INSTANT
COFFEE GRANULES

15ml | 1tbsp BOILING WATER

For the ice cream

4 EGG YOLKS

75g | 3oz | 6 tbsp CASTER SUGAR

5ml | 1 tsp CORNFLOUR

300ml | ½ pint | 1¼ cups
SEMI-SKIMMED MILK

5ml | 1tsp VANILLA ESSENCE

300ml | ½ pint | 1¼ cups
WHIPPING CREAM

1 To make the sauce, put cornflour and a little evaporated milk in a small, heavy-based saucepan and mix to a smooth paste. Add the sugar and remaining evaporated milk. Cook over a gentle heat, stirring until sugar has dissolved, then increase the heat and cook, stirring continuously, until slightly thickened and just beginning to darken in colour.

2 Take the pan off the heat. Mix the coffee with the boiling water and stir into the sauce. Cool the sauce quickly by plunging the base of the pan into cold water.

3 Whisk the egg yolks, sugar and cornflour together until thick and foaming. Bring milk just to the boil in a heavy-based saucepan then gradually whisk into the yolk mixture. Return to the pan and cook over a gentle heat, stirring continuously until thickened and smooth. Pour back into the bowl, stir in vanilla and leave to cool.

4 BY HAND: Whip the cream until thickened but still soft enough to fall from a spoon. Fold into custard then pour into a plastic container and freeze for 4 hours, beating once, halfway through, with a fork, electric whisk or food processor.

USING AN ICE CREAM MAKER: Mix the custard and cream together and churn until thick but not firm enough to scoop.

5 BY HAND: Beat the ice cream again to break up any ice crystals.

USING AN ICE CREAM MAKER: Transfer the semi-frozen churned ice cream to a plastic container.

6 Beat the toffee sauce well and drizzle it thickly over the ice cream. Marble together by roughly running a knife through the mixture. Cover and freeze the ice cream for 4-5 hours until it is firm enough to scoop. Serve in scoops in bowls or plates.

COOK'S TIP *If the sauce is too thick to drizzle, gently warm the base of the pan for a few seconds, stirring well.*

VARIATION *The sauce is also delicious drizzled over plain vanilla ice cream.*

fruit & nut
ice creams

From classic fruit-flavoured ice creams to those speckled with roughly chopped toasted nuts, this chapter imaginatively introduces the most widely used ice cream flavours. Fresh fruit purées, liqueured dried fruits and satisfying nuts transform a basic ice cream into something very special.

Simple Strawberry Ice Cream

Capture the essence of childhood summers with this easy-to-make ice cream.
Whipping cream is better than double cream for this recipe as
it doesn't overwhelm the taste of the fresh fruit.

SERVES FOUR TO SIX

INGREDIENTS

500g | 1¼lb | 4 cups
STRAWBERRIES, hulled

50g | 2oz | ½ cup ICING SUGAR

juice of ½ LEMON

300ml | ½ pint | 1¼ cups
WHIPPING CREAM

extra STRAWBERRIES,
to decorate

1 Purée the strawberries in a food processor or blender until smooth then add the icing sugar and lemon juice and process again to mix. Press the purée through a sieve into a bowl. Chill until very cold.

2 BY HAND: Whip the cream until it is just thickened but still falls from a spoon. Fold into the purée, then pour into a plastic tub or similar freezerproof container. Freeze for 6 hours until firm, beating twice with a fork, electric whisk or in a food processor to break up the ice crystals.

USING AN ICE CREAM MAKER: Churn the purée until mushy, then pour in the cream and churn until thick enough to scoop. Scoop into dishes and decorate with a few extra strawberries.

COOK'S TIP *If possible, taste the strawberries before buying them. Halve large strawberries for decoration.*

VARIATION *Raspberry or any other berry fruit can be used to make this ice cream, in the same way as strawberry.*

Gooseberry and Clotted Cream Ice Cream

Often a rather neglected fruit, conjuring up images of the tired grey-looking crumble that used to be served at school or in the works canteen. This indulgent ice cream puts gooseberries in a totally different class. Its delicious, slightly tart flavour goes particularly well with tiny, melt-in-the-mouth meringues.

SERVES FOUR TO SIX

INGREDIENTS

500g | 1¼lb | 4 cups GOOSEBERRIES, topped and tailed

60ml | 4 tbsp WATER

75g | 3oz | 6 tbsp CASTER SUGAR

150ml | ¼ pint | ⅔ cup WHIPPING CREAM

a few drops of GREEN FOOD COLOURING (optional)

120ml | 4fl oz | ½ cup CLOTTED CREAM

FRESH MINT SPRIGS, to decorate

MERINGUES, to serve

1 Put the gooseberries in a saucepan and add the water and sugar. Cover and simmer for 10 minutes or until soft. Tip into a food processor or blender and process to a smooth purée. Press through a sieve placed over a bowl. Cool, then chill.

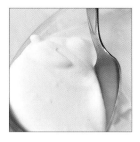

2 BY HAND: Chill the purée in a plastic tub or similar container. Whip the cream until it is thick but still falls from a spoon. Fold into the purée with the green food colouring, if using. Freeze for 2 hours, then beat with a fork, electric mixer or in a food processor, to break up. Return to the freezer for 2 hours.

3 BY HAND: Beat the ice cream again, then fold in the clotted cream. Freeze for 2–3 hours.

USING AN ICE CREAM MAKER: Mix the chilled purée with the whipping cream, add a few drops of green food colouring if using and churn until thickened and semi-frozen. Add the clotted cream and continue to churn until thick enough to scoop.

4 To serve, scoop the ice cream into dishes or small plates, decorate with fresh mint sprigs and add a few small meringues to each serving.

COOK'S TIP *Just a small amount of clotted cream adds a surprising richness to this simple ice cream. If the gooseberry purée is very tart, you can add extra sugar when mixing in the whipping cream.*

Blackberry Ice Cream

There could scarcely be fewer ingredients in this delicious, vibrant ice cream. If you make the ice cream in a machine, don't be tempted to add the cream with the fruit or the mixture will become buttery by the time it has been churned and is stiff enough to scoop.

SERVES FOUR TO SIX

INGREDIENTS

500g | 1¼lb | 5 cups BLACKBERRIES, hulled, plus extra, to decorate

75g | 3oz | 6 tbsp CASTER SUGAR

30ml | 2 tbsp WATER

300ml | ½ pint | 1¼ cups WHIPPING CREAM

CRISP DESSERT BISCUITS, to serve

1 Put the blackberries into a pan, and add the sugar and water. Cover and simmer for 5 minutes until just soft.

2 Tip the fruit into a sieve placed over a bowl and press it through the mesh, using a wooden spoon. Leave to cool, then chill.

3 BY HAND: Whip the cream until it is just thick but still soft enough to fall from a spoon, then mix it with the chilled fruit purée. Pour the mixture into a plastic tub or similar freezerproof container and freeze for 2 hours.

USING AN ICE CREAM MAKER: Churn the chilled purée for 10–15 minutes until it is thick, then gradually pour in the cream. There is no need to whip the cream first.

4 BY HAND: Mash the mixture with a fork, or beat it in a food processor to break up the ice crystals. Return it to the freezer for 4 hours more, beating the mixture again after 2 hours.

USING AN ICE CREAM MAKER: Continue to churn the ice cream until it is firm enough to scoop.

5 Scoop into dishes and decorate with extra blackberries. Serve with crisp dessert biscuits.

VARIATION *Frozen blackberries can be used for the purée. You will need to increase the cooking time to 10 minutes and stir occasionally. Blackcurrants can be used instead of blackberries. A combination of blackberries and peeled and sliced cooking apples also works well.*

Banana and Toffee Ice Cream

The addition of sweetened condensed milk helps to bring out the natural flavour of the bananas and, surprisingly, the ice cream is not excessively sweet.

SERVES FOUR TO SIX

INGREDIENTS

3 RIPE BANANAS

juice of 1 LEMON

370g | 12½oz can SWEETENED CONDENSED MILK

150ml | ¼ pint | ⅔ cup WHIPPING CREAM

150g | 5oz TOFFEES

chopped TOFFEES, to decorate

1 Process the bananas to a purée in a food processor or blender, then add the lemon juice and process briefly to mix. Scrape the purée into a plastic tub or similar freezerproof container.

2 Pour in the condensed milk, stirring with a metal spoon, then add the cream. Mix well, cover and freeze for 4 hours or until mushy.

3 Unwrap the toffees and chop them finely, using a sharp knife. If this proves difficult, put them in a double plastic bag and hit them with a rolling pin.

4 Beat the semi-frozen ice cream with a fork or electric mixer to break up the ice crystals, then stir in the toffees. Return the ice cream to the freezer for 3–5 hours or until firm. Scoop on to a plate or into a bowl and decorate with chopped toffees. Serve at once.

COOK'S TIP *Because of the consistency of the sweetened condensed milk this ice cream takes a long time to freeze and is best made by hand rather than by machine. To reduce the initial freezing time, start chilling the mixture in a stainless steel roasting tin, transferring to a plastic tub only after adding the toffees. If you are making this ice cream for small children, you may prefer to leave the toffees out or use chopped chocolate instead.*

Apricot and Amaretti Ice Cream

Prolong the very short season of fresh apricots by transforming them into this superb ice cream with crushed amaretti biscuits and whipped cream.

SERVES FOUR TO SIX

INGREDIENTS

500g | 1¼lb FRESH APRICOTS, halved and stoned

juice of 1 ORANGE

50g | 2oz | ¼ cup CASTER SUGAR

300ml | ½ pint | 1¼ cups WHIPPING CREAM

50g | 2oz AMARETTI BISCUITS

1 Put the apricots, orange juice and sugar in a saucepan. Cover and simmer for 5 minutes until the fruit is tender. Leave to cool.

2 Lift out one third of the fruit and set it aside on a plate. Tip the remaining contents of the pan into a food processor or blender and process to a smooth purée.

3 BY HAND: Whip the cream until it is just thick but still soft enough to fall from a spoon. Gradually add the fruit purée, folding it into the mixture. Pour into a plastic tub or similar freezerproof container and freeze for 4 hours, beating once with a fork, electric mixer or in a food processor.

USING AN ICE CREAM MAKER: Churn the apricot purée until it is slushy, then gradually add the cream. Continue to churn until the ice cream is thick, but not firm enough to scoop.

4 BY HAND: Beat for a second time. Crumble in the amaretti biscuits.

USING AN ICE CREAM MAKER: Scrape the ice cream into a tub. Crumble in the amaretti biscuits.

5 Add the reserved apricots and gently fold these ingredients into the ice cream. Freeze for 2–3 hours or until firm enough to scoop.

COOK'S TIP *Chill the fruit purée if you have time; this will speed up the churning or freezing process. If you have some amaretto liqueur, fold in 45ml / 3 tbsp with the biscuits.*

Peach and Cardamom Yogurt Ice

SERVES FOUR

The velvety texture of this smooth peach ice cream spiced with cardamom suggests it is made with cream, but the secret ingredient is actually natural yogurt; great for those watching their waistline.

INGREDIENTS

8 CARDAMOM PODS

6 PEACHES,
total weight about 500g | 1¼lb,
halved, and stoned

75g | 3oz | 6 tbsp CASTER SUGAR

30ml | 2 tbsp WATER

200ml | 7fl oz | scant 1 cup
BIO NATURAL YOGURT

1 Put the cardamom pods on a board and crush them with the bottom of a ramekin, or in a mortar and pestle.

2 Chop the peaches roughly and put them in a saucepan. Add the crushed cardamom pods, with their black seeds, and the sugar and water. Cover and simmer for 10 minutes or until the fruit is tender. Leave to cool.

3 Tip the peach mixture into a food processor or blender, process until smooth, then press through a sieve placed over a bowl.

4 BY HAND: Add the yogurt to the sieved purée and mix together in the bowl.

5 BY HAND: Pour into a plastic tub and freeze for 5–6 hours until firm, beating once or twice with a fork, electric whisk or in a processor to break up the ice crystals.

USING AN ICE CREAM MAKER: Churn the purée until thick, then scrape it into a plastic tub or similar container. Stir in the yogurt and freeze until firm enough to hold a scoop shape.

6 Scoop the ice cream on to a large platter, and serve at once.

COOK'S TIP *Use bio natural yogurt for its extra mild taste. Greek yogurt or ordinary natural yogurt are both sharper and more acidic and tend to overwhelm the delicate taste of the peaches. Use a melon baller to make miniature scoops in individual dishes.*

Mango and Passion Fruit Gelato

Fresh and fruity, this tropical ice cream has a delicate perfume.
Passion fruit tend to vary in size. If you can locate the large
ones, four will be plenty for this dish.

SERVES FOUR

INGREDIENTS

4 LARGE MANGOES

grated rind and juice of 1 LIME

50g | 2oz | ¼ cup CASTER SUGAR

300ml | ½ pint | 1¼ cups
WHIPPING CREAM

4–6 PASSION FRUIT

1 Cut a thick slice from either side
of the stone on each unpeeled
mango. Using a sharp knife, make
criss-cross cuts in the mango flesh,
cutting down as far as the skin.

2 Turn the slices inside out so that
the pieces of mango stand proud
of the skin, then scoop them into a
food processor or blender, using a
spoon. Finally, cut the remaining
flesh away from the stones and add
it to the rest.

3 Process the mango flesh until
smooth, then add the grated lime
rind, lime juice and caster sugar
and process briefly.

4 BY HAND: Whip the cream until it
is just thick but will still fall from a
spoon. Fold in the puréed mango
and lime mixture, then pour into a
plastic tub or similar freezerproof
container. Freeze for 4 hours until
semi-frozen.

USING AN ICE CREAM MAKER: Churn
the fruit mixture for 10–15
minutes, then add the cream and
continue to churn until the mixture
is thick but still too soft to scoop.
Scrape it into a plastic tub.

5 Cut the passion fruit in half and
scoop the seeds and pulp into the
ice cream mixture, mix well and
freeze for 2 hours until firm
enough to scoop.

Pineapple Crush

Look out for pineapples that are labelled"extra sweet". This variety has bright sunflower-yellow flesh that is naturally sweet and juicy. It is ideal for making the most wonderful ice cream.

SERVES FOUR TO SIX

INGREDIENTS

2 EXTRA-SWEET PINEAPPLES

300ml | ½ pint | 1¼ cups
WHIPPING CREAM

50g | 2oz | ¼ cup CASTER SUGAR

1 Slice one pineapple in half through the leafy top, then scoop out the flesh from both halves, keeping the shells intact. Stand them upside down to drain, wrap in clear film and chill until needed.

2 Trim the top off the remaining pineapple, cut the flesh into slices, then cut away the skin and any "eyes". Remove the core from each slice, then finely chop the flesh from both pineapples.

3 Purée 300g | 11oz of the pineapple in a food processor or blender. Set aside the remaining chopped pineapple.

4 BY HAND: Whip the cream until it is just thick but still falls from a spoon. Fold in the purée and sugar, then pour into a plastic tub or similar freezerproof container. Freeze for 6 hours, beating twice with a fork, electric mixer or in a food processor.

USING AN ICE CREAM MAKER: Churn the pineapple purée with the sugar for 15–20 minutes. Mix in the cream and churn until thick but still too soft to scoop.

5 BY HAND: Fold in 175g | 6oz | 1½ cups of the chopped pineapple and freeze for 2–3 hours.

USING AN ICE CREAM MAKER: Add the pineapple to the ice cream maker and continue to churn the ice cream until it is stiff enough to serve in scoops.

6 Serve the ice cream in scoops in the pineapple shells. Offer any remaining pineapple separately.

VARIATION *This ice cream is also delicious mixed with meringues: crumble four meringue nests into the ice cream mixture when adding the finely chopped pineapple.*

Apricot Parfait

Pots of creamy, delicately flavoured French-style ice cream conceal a hidden layer of poached apricots. If you don't have time to make the caramel, top each dessert with a spoonful of extra thick double cream and some thin strips of extra apricot.

SERVES SIX

INGREDIENTS

200g | 7oz | scant 1 cup DRIED APRICOTS

300ml | ½ pint | 1¼ cups APPLE JUICE

75g | 3oz | 6 tbsp DEMERARA SUGAR

4 EGG YOLKS

115g | 4oz | generous ½ cup CASTER SUGAR

120ml | 4fl oz | ½ cup WATER

150ml | ¼ pint | ⅔ cup WHIPPING CREAM

grated rind and juice of ½ LEMON

1 Put the apricots in a saucepan. Pour over the apple juice and soak for 3–4 hours. Meanwhile, line a baking sheet with foil. Using an inverted ramekin as a guide, draw six circles on the foil. Brush with a little oil.

2 Preheat the grill to its lowest setting. Sprinkle the demerara sugar into the marked circles. Place under the grill, on its lowest shelf setting and leave for 3–4 minutes until the sugar has dissolved and caramelized. Leave to cool and harden.

3 Simmer the soaked apricots for 10 minutes until they are soft and plump. Leave to cool, then lift out nine apricots with a slotted spoon.

4 Chop these apricots roughly and divide them among six freezerproof ramekins. Purée the remaining apricots and juice until smooth.

5 Whisk the egg yolks in a large, heatproof bowl until frothy. Put the caster sugar and water in a pan, heat gently until the sugar has dissolved, then boil for 4–5 minutes, until the syrup registers 115°C | 239°F on a sugar thermometer. Alternatively, test by dropping a little of the syrup into a cup of cold water. Pour the water away. The syrup should mould into a soft ball.

6 Quickly whisk the hot syrup into the egg yolks. Put the bowl over a saucepan of simmering water and whisk the mixture until it is thick.

7 Lift the bowl off the pan and continue whisking the mixture until it is cool and the whisk leaves a trail when lifted.

8 Whip the cream lightly, fold it into the yolk mixture, then gently fold in the apricot purée, with the lemon rind and juice.

9 Pour the parfait mixture into the six ramekins and freeze for 4 hours until firm. When ready to serve, roughly break the caramelized sugar into chunky pieces and use to decorate the ices.

Rum and Raisin Ice Cream

An old favourite with fathers and grandfathers. For children this ice cream always seemed so much more
sophisticated than mere vanilla. The longer you can leave the raisins to soak in the rum
the stronger the flavour will be.

SERVES FOUR TO SIX

INGREDIENTS

150g | 5oz | scant 1 cup
LARGE RAISINS

60ml | 4 tbsp DARK RUM

4 EGG YOLKS

75g | 3oz | 6 tbsp LIGHT
MUSCOVADO SUGAR

5ml | 1 tsp CORNFLOUR

300ml | ½ pint | 1¼ cups
SEMI-SKIMMED MILK

300ml | ½ pint | 1¼ cups
WHIPPING CREAM

DESSERT BISCUITS or
ICE CREAM CONES, to serve

4 BY HAND: Whip the cream until it is just thick but still falls from a spoon. Fold it into the custard and pour the mixture into a plastic tub or similar freezerproof container. Freeze for 4 hours, beating once with a fork, electric mixer or in a food processor. Then beat again.

USING AN ICE CREAM MAKER: Pour the cream into the custard, then churn until thick. Transfer to a plastic container.

1 Put the raisins in a bowl, add the rum and mix well. Cover and leave to soak for 3–4 hours or overnight if possible.

2 Whisk the egg yolks, muscovado sugar and cornflour in a large bowl until the mixture is thick and foamy. Pour the milk into a heavy-based saucepan, and bring it to just below boiling point.

3 Gradually whisk the milk into the eggs, then pour the mixture back into the pan. Cook over a gentle heat, stirring constantly until the custard thickens and is smooth. Take off the heat and leave to cool.

5 Fold the soaked raisins into the ice cream, cover and freeze for 2–3 hours or until firm enough to scoop. Serve in bowls or tall glasses with dessert biscuits, or serve simply in ice cream cones.

COOK'S TIP *If you scoop it into cones, the ice cream will serve 6–8 people. If you haven't any dark rum, white rum, brandy or even whisky can be used instead.*

Rhubarb and Ginger Ice Cream

A fruit so highly favoured by Queen Victoria; two varieties of rhubarb were grown and named after her and her consort Prince Albert. The classic combination of gently poached rhubarb and chopped ginger is brought up to date by blending it with mascarpone to make this pretty blush-pink ice cream.

SERVES FOUR TO SIX

INGREDIENTS

5 pieces of STEM GINGER

450g | 1lb trimmed RHUBARB, sliced

115g | 4oz | ½ cup CASTER SUGAR

30ml | 2 tbsp WATER

150g | 5oz | ⅔ cup MASCARPONE

150ml | ¼ pint | ⅔ cup WHIPPING CREAM

WAFER CUPS, to serve (optional)

VARIATION *If the rhubarb purée is rather pale, add a few drops of pink colouring when mixing in the cream.*

1 Using a sharp knife, roughly chop the stem ginger and set it aside. Put the rhubarb slices into a saucepan and add the sugar and water. Cover and simmer for 5 minutes until the rhubarb is just tender and still bright pink.

2 Tip the mixture into a food processor or blender, process until smooth, then leave to cool. Chill if time permits.

3 BY HAND: Mix together the mascarpone, cream and ginger with the rhubarb purée.

USING AN ICE CREAM MAKER: Churn the rhubarb purée for 15–20 minutes until it is thick.

4 BY HAND: Pour the mixture into a plastic tub or similar freezerproof container and freeze for 6 hours or until firm, beating once or twice during the freezing time to break up the ice crystals.

USNG AN ICE CREAM MAKER: Put the mascarpone into a bowl, soften it with a wooden spoon, then gradually beat in the cream. Add the chopped ginger, then transfer to the ice cream maker and churn until the ice cream is firm. Serve as scoops in bowls or wafer baskets.

Nougat Ice Cream

Taking its inspiration from the delicious sweetmeats served in France as one of the 13 traditional Christmas desserts, this is a superb ice cream, especially when served with iced liqueurs as iced petits fours.

SERVES SIX TO EIGHT

INGREDIENTS

50g | 2oz | ½ cup HAZELNUTS

50g | 2oz | ½ cup PISTACHIO NUTS

50g | 2oz | ⅓ cup CANDIED PEEL, in large pieces

6–8 sheets RICE PAPER

3 EGG WHITES

150g | 5oz | 1¼ cups ICING SUGAR, sifted

300ml | ½ pint | 1¼ cups DOUBLE CREAM

10ml | 2 tsp ORANGE FLOWER WATER

1 Spread out the hazelnuts on a baking sheet and brown them lightly under a hot grill. Mix them with the pistachios and chop all the nuts roughly. Slice the candied peel thinly then cut the slices into bite-size slivers.

2 Line the base and sides of a 28 x 18 x 4cm | 11 x 7 x 1½in cake tin with clear film, then with four of the pieces of rice paper, folding the paper into the corners and overlapping the sheets slightly.

3 Put the egg whites and icing sugar into a large, heatproof bowl. Place it over a saucepan of simmering water and whisk for 5 minutes or until the meringue is very thick.

4 Take off the heat and continue whisking until soft peaks form. In a separate bowl, whip the cream and orange flower water lightly, then fold in the meringue.

5 Spoon half the meringue mixture into the lined cake tin, easing it into the corners.

6 Sprinkle the meringue with half the nuts and candied peel. Cover with the remaining meringue mixture.

7 Sprinkle with the remaining nuts and fruit. Cover with two more sheets of rice paper and freeze for at least 6 hours or overnight until completely firm.

8 Carefully turn the ice cream out of the tin and peel off the clear film. If the base of the ice cream is soft, cover it with the remaining two sheets of rice paper, pressing it on to the ice cream so that it sticks. Cut into small squares or triangles, arrange on individual plates and serve.

VARIATION *Use toasted blanched almonds instead of pistachios if you prefer. The meringue can be flavoured with rose water or grated lemon rind instead of orange flower water.*

Maple and Pecan Nut Ice Cream

This all-American ice cream is even more delicious when it is served with extra maple syrup and topped with whole pecan nuts.

SERVES FOUR TO SIX

INGREDIENTS

115g | 4oz | 1 cup PECAN NUTS

4 EGG YOLKS

50g | 2oz | ¼ cup CASTER SUGAR

5ml | 1 tsp CORNFLOUR

300ml | ½ pint | 1¼ cups
SEMI-SKIMMED MILK

60ml | 4 tbsp MAPLE SYRUP

300ml | ½ pint | 1¼ cups
WHIPPING CREAM

extra MAPLE SYRUP AND PECAN
NUTS, to serve

1 Cut the pecan nuts in half lengthways, spread them out on a baking sheet and grill them under a moderate heat for 2–3 minutes until lightly browned. Remove from the heat and leave to cool.

2 Place the egg yolks, sugar and cornflour into a bowl and whisk until thick and foamy. Pour the milk into a heavy-based saucepan, bring to the boil, then gradually whisk it into the yolk mixture.

3 Return the mixture to the pan and cook over a gentle heat, stirring constantly until the custard thickens and is smooth.

4 Pour the custard back into the bowl, and stir in the maple syrup. Leave to cool, then chill.

5 BY HAND: Whip the cream until it is thick but still falls from a spoon. Fold it into the custard and pour into a plastic tub or similar freezerproof container. Freeze for 4 hours, beating once with a fork, electric mixer or in a food processor to break up the ice crystals. After this time, beat it again.

USING AN ICE CREAM MAKER: Stir the cream into the custard, then churn the mixture until thick. Scrape into a plastic container.

6 Fold in the nuts. Freeze for 2–3 hours until firm enough to scoop into dishes. Pour extra maple syrup over each portion and top with extra pecan nuts.

COOK'S TIP *Avoid "maple-flavoured" syrup, the flavour is harsher and tends to taste rather synthetic. Look out for "pure maple syrup" on the label.*

Rocky Road Ice Cream

This American classic ice cream is a mouth-watering combination of roughly crushed praline, rich vanilla custard and whipping cream.

SERVES FOUR TO SIX

INGREDIENTS

4 EGG YOLKS

5ml | 1 tsp CORNFLOUR

225g | 8oz | generous 1 cup GRANULATED SUGAR

300ml | ½ pint | 1¼ cups SEMI-SKIMMED MILK

10ml | 2 tsp NATURAL VANILLA ESSENCE

OIL, for greasing

50g | 2oz | ½ cup MACADAMIA NUTS

50g | 2oz | ½ cup HAZELNUTS

50g | 2oz | ½ cup FLAKED ALMONDS

60ml | 4 tbsp WATER

300ml | ½ pint | 1¼ cups WHIPPING CREAM

1 Put the egg yolks in a bowl and stir in the cornflour, with 75g | 3oz | 6 tbsp of the sugar. Whisk until the mixture has turned thick and foamy. Pour the milk into a heavy-based saucepan, bring it to the boil, then gradually whisk it into the yolk mixture in the bowl.

2 Return the mixture to the pan. Cook over a gentle heat, stirring constantly until the custard thickens and is smooth. Pour it back into the bowl and stir in the natural vanilla essence. Leave to cool, then chill.

3 Grease a large baking sheet with oil. Put the remaining sugar in a large, heavy-based frying pan, sprinkle the nuts on top and pour over the water. Heat gently, without stirring, until the sugar has dissolved completely, then boil the syrup for 3–5 minutes until it is just beginning to turn golden.

4 Quickly pour the nut mixture on to the oiled baking sheet and leave to cool and harden.

5 BY HAND: Whip the cream until it is thick but still falls from a spoon. Fold it into the custard and pour into a plastic tub or similar freezerproof container. Freeze for 4 hours, beating once with a fork, electric mixer or in a food processor and then beat it again.

USING AN ICE CREAM MAKER: Stir the cream into the custard and churn until stiff but too soft to scoop. Scrape into a tub.

6 Smash the praline with a rolling pin to break off about a third. Reserve this for the decoration. Put the rest of the praline into a strong plastic bag and hit it several times with a rolling pin until it breaks into bite-size pieces.

7 Fold the crushed praline into the ice cream and freeze it for 2–3 hours until firm. Scoop into glasses and decorate with the reserved praline, broken into large pieces.

COOK'S TIP *If you can't locate macadamia nuts, use extra hazelnuts. If the nuts fail to brown evenly when you are making the praline in the frying pan, don't stir the syrup. Instead, tilt the pan first one way then the other.*

Cashew and Orange Flower Ice Cream

Delicately perfumed with orange flower water and a little orange rind, this nutty, lightly sweetened ice cream evokes images of puddings that are popular in the Middle East.

4 Stir the orange flower water and grated orange rind into the chilled custard. Process the nut cream in a food processor or blender until it forms a fine paste, then stir it into the custard mixture.

SERVES FOUR TO SIX

INGREDIENTS

4 EGG YOLKS

75g | 3oz | 6 tbsp CASTER SUGAR

5ml | 1 tsp CORNFLOUR

300ml | ½ pint | 1¼ cups
SEMI-SKIMMED MILK

300ml | ½ pint | 1¼ cups
WHIPPING CREAM

150g | 5oz | 1¼ cups CASHEW NUTS,
finely chopped

15ml | 1 tbsp ORANGE FLOWER
WATER

grated rind of ½ ORANGE,
plus CURLS OF THINLY PARED
ORANGE RIND, to decorate

1 Whisk the egg yolks, caster sugar and cornflour in a bowl until thick and foamy. Pour the semi-skimmed milk into a heavy-based saucepan, gently bring it to the boil, then gradually whisk it into the egg yolk mixture.

2 Return to the pan and cook over a gentle heat, stirring constantly until smooth. Pour back into the bowl. Cool, then chill.

3 Heat the cream in a saucepan. When it boils, stir in the chopped cashew nuts. Leave to cool.

5 BY HAND: Pour the mixture into a plastic tub or similar freezerproof container and freeze for 6 hours, beating twice with a fork or whisk with an electric mixer to break up the ice crystals.

USING AN ICE CREAM MAKER:
Churn the mixture until it is firm enough to scoop.

6 To serve, scoop the ice cream into dishes and decorate each portion with an orange rind curl.

COOK'S TIP *For a more intense flavour, roast the cashew nuts before chopping them. Thinly pare the orange rind, then wrap each strip in turn around a cocktail stick and leave it for a minute or two.*

Pistachio Ice Cream

This continental favourite owes its enduring popularity to its delicate pale green colour and distinctive yet subtle flavour. Buy the pistachio nuts as you need them as they quickly go stale if left in the cupboard.

SERVES FOUR TO SIX

INGREDIENTS

4 EGG YOLKS

75g | 3oz | 6 tbsp CASTER SUGAR

5ml | 1 tsp CORNFLOUR

300ml | ½ pint | 1¼ cups
SEMI-SKIMMED MILK

115g | 4oz | 1 cup PISTACHIOS, plus a
few extra, to decorate

300ml | ½ pint | 1¼ cups
WHIPPING CREAM

a little GREEN FOOD COLOURING

CHOCOLATE DIPPED WAFFLE
CONES, to serve (optional)

1 Place the egg yolks, sugar and cornflour in a bowl and whisk until the mixture is thick and foamy.

2 Pour the milk into a heavy-based saucepan, gently bring it to the boil, then gradually whisk it into the egg yolk mixture.

3 Return the mixture to the saucepan and cook it over a gentle heat, stirring constantly until the custard thickens and is smooth. Pour it back into the bowl, set aside to cool, then chill in the refrigerator until required.

4 Shell the pistachios and put them in a food processor or blender. Add 30ml | 2 tbsp of the cream and grind the mixture to a coarse paste.

5 Pour the rest of the cream into a small saucepan. Bring it to the boil, stir in the coarsely ground pistachios, then leave to cool.

6 Mix the chilled custard and pistachio cream together and tint the mixture delicately with a few drops of food colouring.

7 BY HAND: Pour the tinted custard and pistachio mixture into a plastic tub or similar freezerproof container. Freeze for 6 hours, beating once or twice with a fork or in an electric mixer to break up the ice crystals. Scoop the ice cream into cones or dishes to serve and sprinkle each portion with a few extra pistachios.

USING AN ICE CREAM MAKER: Churn the mixture until firm enough to scoop. Serve in cones or dishes, sprinkled with extra pistachios.

COOK'S TIP *If you make the ice cream by hand, it is important not to beat the frozen mixture in a food processor or the pistachios will become too finely ground. Bought waffle cones can be decorated by dipping them in melted chocolate and sprinkling them with extra chopped pistachios.*

cream-free
&low-fat ices

Whether for dietary reasons or simply through choice, many people do not like to indulge in rich traditional ice creams. On the following pages are some intensely flavoured desserts using low-fat and dairy-free ingredients. With recipes that range from a smooth creamy coconut ice to a refreshing orange and yogurt ice cream, there is an iced dessert to suit everyone.

Kulfi

This famous Indian ice cream is traditionally made by slowly boiling milk until it has reduced to about one third of the original quantity. Although you can save time by using condensed milk, nothing beats this delicious ice cream when made in the authentic manner.

SERVES FOUR

INGREDIENTS

1.5 litres | 2½ pints | 6¼ cups
FULL-FAT MILK

3 CARDAMOM PODS

25g | 1oz | 2 tbsp CASTER SUGAR

50g | 2oz | ½ cup PISTACHIOS,
skinned plus a few to decorate

a few PINK ROSE PETALS,
to decorate

1 Pour the milk into a large, heavy-based saucepan. Bring to the boil, lower the heat and simmer gently for 1 hour, stirring occasionally.

2 Put the cardamom pods in a mortar and crush them with a pestle. Add the pods and the seeds to the milk and continue to simmer for 1–1½ hours or until the milk has reduced to about 475ml | 16fl oz | 2 cups.

3 Strain the milk into a jug, stir in the sugar and leave to cool.

4 Grind half the pistachios to a smooth powder in a blender, nut grinder or cleaned coffee grinder. Cut the remaining pistachios into thin slivers and set them aside for decoration. Stir the ground nuts into the milk mixture.

5 Pour the milk and pistachio mixture into four kulfi moulds. Freeze overnight until firm.

6 To unmould the kulfi, half fill a plastic container or bowl with very hot water, stand the moulds in the water and count to ten. Immediately lift out the moulds and invert them on a baking sheet.

7 Transfer the ice creams to a platter or individual plates. To decorate, scatter sliced pistachios over the ice creams and then the rose petals. Serve at once.

COOK'S TIP *Stay in the kitchen while the milk is simmering, so that you can control the heat to keep the milk gently bubbling without boiling over. If you don't have any kulfi moulds, use lolly moulds without the tops or even disposable plastic cups. If the ices won't turn out, dip a cloth in very hot water, wring it out and place it on the tops of the moulds to soften the ice cream, or plunge the moulds back into hot water for a few more seconds.*

Dondurma Kaymalki

This sweet, pure white ice cream comes from the Middle East, where it is traditionally thickened with sahlab and flavoured with orange flower water and mastic, a resin used in chewing gum. As sahlab and mastic are both difficult to obtain in the West, cornflour and condensed milk have been used in their place.

SERVES FOUR TO SIX

INGREDIENTS

45ml | 3 tbsp CORNFLOUR

600ml | 1 pint | 2½ cups
FULL-FAT MILK

213g | 7½oz can SWEETENED
CONDENSED MILK

15ml | 1 tbsp CLEAR HONEY

10ml | 2 tsp ORANGE
FLOWER WATER

a few SUGARED ALMONDS,
to serve

1 Put the cornflour in a saucepan and mix to a smooth paste with a little of the milk. Stir in the remaining milk and the condensed milk and bring the mixture to the boil, stirring until it has thickened and is smooth. Pour the mixture into a bowl.

2 Stir in the honey and orange flower water. Cover with a plate to prevent the formation of a skin, leave to cool, then chill.

3 BY HAND: Pour the mixture into a plastic tub or similar freezerproof container and freeze for 6–8 hours, beating twice with a fork, electric mixer or in a food processor to break up the ice crystals.

USING AN ICE CREAM MAKER: Churn until firm enough to scoop.

4 To serve, scoop into dishes and serve with a few sugared almonds.

VARIATION *Rose water can be used instead of orange flower water. If you have made the ice cream by hand, remember to transfer it to the fridge about half an hour before you are ready to scoop.*

Date and Tofu Ice

All you sceptics who claim to hate tofu, prepare to be converted by this creamy date and apple ice cream.

Generously spiced with cinnamon, it not only tastes good but is packed with soya protein,

contains no added sugar, is low in fat and free from all dairy products.

SERVES FOUR

INGREDIENTS

250g | 9oz | 1½ cups STONED DATES

600ml | 1 pint | 2½ cups APPLE JUICE

5ml | 1 tsp GROUND CINNAMON

285g | 10½oz pack CHILLED TOFU,
drained and cubed

150ml | ¼ pint | ⅔ cup
UNSWEETENED SOYA MILK

1 Put the dates in a saucepan. Pour in 300ml | ½ pint | 1¼ cups of the apple juice and leave to soak for 2 hours. Simmer for 10 minutes, then leave to cool. Using a slotted spoon, lift out one-quarter of the dates, chop roughly and set aside.

2 Purée the remaining dates in a food processor or blender. Add the cinnamon and process with enough of the remaining apple juice to make a smooth paste.

3 Add the cubes of tofu, a few at a time, processing after each addition. Finally, add the remaining apple juice and the soya milk.

4 BY HAND: Pour the mixture into a plastic tub or similar freezerproof container and freeze for 4 hours, beating once with a fork, electric mixer or in a food processor to break up the ice crystals. After this time, beat again with a fork to ensure a smooth texture.

USING AN ICE CREAM MAKER: Churn the mixture until very thick, but not thick enough to scoop. Scrape into a plastic tub.

5 Stir in most of the chopped dates and freeze for 2–3 hours until firm.

6 Scoop into dessert glasses and decorate with the remaining chopped dates.

COOK'S TIP *As tofu is a non-dairy product it will not blend completely, so don't be concerned if the mixture contains tiny flecks of tofu.*

Coconut Ice

Despite its creamy taste, this ice cream contains neither cream nor egg and is very refreshing. Serve it with scoops of Red Berry Sorbet.

SERVES FOUR TO SIX

INGREDIENTS

150ml | ¼ pint | ⅔ cup WATER

115g | 4oz | ½ cup CASTER SUGAR

2 LIMES

400ml | 14fl oz can COCONUT MILK

TOASTED COCONUT SHAVINGS, to decorate (see Cook's Tip)

1 Put the water in a small saucepan. Tip in the caster sugar and bring to the boil, stirring constantly until the sugar has all dissolved. Remove the pan from the heat and leave the syrup to cool, then chill well.

2 Grate the limes finely, taking care to avoid the bitter pith. Squeeze them and pour the juice and rind into the pan of syrup. Add the coconut milk.

3 BY HAND: Pour the mixture into a plastic tub or similar freezerproof container and freeze for 5–6 hours until firm, beating twice with a fork, electric whisk or in a food processor to break up the crystals. Scoop into dishes and decorate with toasted coconut shavings.

ICE CREAM MAKER: Churn the mixture until firm enough to scoop. Serve in dishes, decorated with the toasted coconut shavings.

COOK'S TIP *Use the flesh from a coconut to make a pretty decoration. Having rinsed the flesh with cold water, cut off thin slices using a swivel-bladed vegetable peeler. Toast the slices under a moderate grill until the coconut has curled and the edges have turned golden. Cool slightly, then sprinkle the shavings over the coconut ice.*

Banana Gelato

This mild, creamy banana ice cream is made with soya milk, making it good for children who are lactose intolerant or allergic to dairy products.

SERVES FOUR TO SIX

INGREDIENTS

115g | 4oz | ½ cup CASTER SUGAR

150ml | ¼ pint | ⅔ cup WATER

1 LEMON

3 RIPE BANANAS

300ml | ½ pint | 1¼ cups
UHT VANILLA-FLAVOURED
SOYA DESSERT

1 Put the sugar and water in a saucepan and bring to the boil, stirring until the sugar has dissolved. Set the syrup aside to cool.

2 Squeeze the lemon. Put the bananas in a bowl and mash with a fork. Slowly add the lemon juice.

3 BY HAND: Stir in the cooled sugar syrup and the vanilla-flavoured soya dessert. Pour the mixture into a large plastic container and freeze for 6–7 hours until firm, beating twice during that time with a fork, electric mixer or in a food processor to break up the ice crystals. Scoop into dishes and serve.

USING AN ICE CREAM MAKER: Stir in the cooled sugar syrup and the soya dessert. Churn the mixture until thick, then scrape it into a freezerproof container and freeze for 3–4 hours until firm. Scoop into dishes and serve.

COOK'S TIP *This recipe makes 1 litre | 1¾ pints | 4 cups of frozen gelato, so if you are using an ice cream maker with only a small capacity it may be wise to churn the mixture in two batches. Check your manufacturer's handbook.*

Honeyed Goat's Milk Gelato

Goat's milk is more widely available than it used to be and is more easily tolerated by some individuals than cow's milk. It makes a surprisingly rich iced dessert.

SERVES FOUR

INGREDIENTS

6 EGG YOLKS

50g | 2oz | ¼ cup CASTER SUGAR

10ml | 2 tsp CORNFLOUR

600ml | 1 pint | 2½ cups
GOAT'S MILK

60ml | 4 tbsp CLEAR HONEY

POMEGRANATE SEEDS, to decorate

1 Whisk the egg yolks, sugar and cornflour in a bowl until pale and thick. Pour the goat's milk into a heavy-based saucepan, bring it to the boil, and then gradually whisk it into the yolk mixture.

2 Return the custard mixture to the saucepan and cook over a gentle heat, stirring constantly until the custard thickens and is smooth. Pour it back into the clean bowl.

3 Stir the honey into the milk mixture. Leave to cool, then chill.

4 BY HAND: Pour the mixture into a plastic tub or similar freezerproof container and freeze for 6 hours until firm enough to scoop, beating twice with a fork, electric whisk or in a food processor to break up the ice crystals.

USING AN ICE CREAM MAKER: Churn the chilled mixture until thick enough to scoop.

5 To serve, scoop into dessert glasses and decorate with a few pomegranate seeds.

COOK'S TIP *Make sure the spoon measures are level or the honey flavour will be too dominant.*

VARIATION *This ice cream is also delicious with a little ginger; stir in 40g | 1½oz | ¼ cup finely chopped stem ginger when the ice cream is partially frozen.*

Raspberry Sherbet

Traditional sherbets are made in much the same way as sorbets but with added milk. This modern low fat version is made from raspberry purée blended with sugar syrup and virtually fat free fromage frais, then flecked with crushed raspberries.

SERVES SIX

INGREDIENTS

175g | 6oz | ¾ cup CASTER SUGAR

150ml | ¼ pint | ⅔ cup WATER

500g | 1¼lb | 3½ cups RASPBERRIES, plus extra, to serve

500ml | 17fl oz | generous 2 cups VIRTUALLY FAT-FREE FROMAGE FRAIS

1 Put the sugar and water in a small saucepan and bring to the boil, stirring until the sugar has dissolved. Pour into a jug and cool.

2 Put 350g | 12oz | 2½ cups of the raspberries in a food processor or blender. Process to a purée, then press through a sieve placed over a large bowl to remove the seeds. Stir the sugar syrup into the raspberry purée and chill the mixture until it is very cold.

3 Add the fromage frais to the purée and whisk until smooth.

4 BY HAND: Pour the mixture into a plastic tub or similar freezerproof container and freeze for 4 hours, beating once with a fork, electric whisk or in a food processor to break up the ice crystals. After this time, beat it again.

USING AN ICE CREAM MAKER: Churn the mixture until it is thick but too soft to scoop. Scrape into a freezerproof container.

5 Crush the remaining raspberries between your fingers and add them to the partially frozen ice cream. Mix lightly then freeze for 2–3 hours until firm. Scoop the ice cream into dishes and serve with extra raspberries.

COOK'S TIP *If you intend to make this in an ice cream maker, check your handbook before you begin churning as this recipes makes 900ml | 1½ pints | 3¾ cups of mixture. If this is too large a quantity for your machine, make it in two batches or by hand.*

Orange and Yogurt Ice

Serve this refreshing low-fat yogurt ice simply, in cones, or scoop it into bought meringue baskets and decorate it with blueberries and mint for a more sophisticated treat.

3 BY HAND: Spoon the yogurt into a bowl, gradually add the chilled orange juice and syrup mixture and mix well. Pour the mixture into a plastic tub. Freeze for 6 hours or until firm, beating twice with a fork or in a food processor to break up the ice crystals.

USING AN ICE CREAM MAKER: Churn the orange mixture until thick, but not thick enough to scoop. Switch off the machine, remove the paddle, if necessary, add the yogurt and mix well. Replace the paddle and continue to churn the ice cream for 15–20 minutes until thick. Scrape it into a plastic tub or similar freezerproof container and freeze until firm.

4 Scoop the yogurt ice into cones or meringue nests and decorate with blueberries and mint.

SERVES SIX

INGREDIENTS

90ml | 6 tbsp WATER

10ml | 2 tsp POWDERED GELATINE

115g | 4oz | ½ cup CASTER SUGAR

250ml | 8fl oz | 1 cup "FRESHLY SQUEEZED" ORANGE JUICE from a carton or bottle

500ml | 17fl oz | generous 2 cups BIO YOGURT

CONES or MERINGUE NESTS, BLUEBERRIES and FRESH MINT SPRIGS, to serve

1 Put 30ml | 2 tbsp of the water in a small bowl and sprinkle the powdered gelatine over the top. Set aside until spongy. Meanwhile, put the sugar in a small saucepan, add the remaining water and heat through gently until the sugar has dissolved completely.

2 Take off the heat, add the gelatine and stir until dissolved. Cool, stir in the orange juice and chill for 15–30 minutes.

COOK'S TIP *Meringue nests are not difficult to make, but if you do not have the time, bought ones are a perfectly acceptable alternative.*

Bibliography

Mrs Mary Eales Receipts (1718. Prospect Books, London, reproduced from the 1733 edition.)

Marshall, A.B. *The Book of Ices* (Marshall's, London 1885)

Paul, Charlie. *American and other Iced Drinks* (Farrow and Jackson, London 1909)

Herman Senn, C. *Luncheon and Dinner Sweets including the Art of Ice Making* (Ward Lock 1919)

The History of Ice Cream (International Association of Ice Cream Manufacturers, Washington DC 1978)

Extracts from Petits Propos Culinaires 3rd November 1979
Stallings, W.S. Jr. *Ice Cream and Water Ices in 17th- and 18th-century England*
David, Elizabeth. (articles in the same journal)

The Great Ice Cream Book, edited by Edwards, R. and Croft, J. (Absolute Press 1984)

Beamon, Sylvia P. and Roaf, Susan. *The Ice Houses of Britain* (Routledge 1990)

Copi, Terri. *The Italian Factor: The Italian Community in Great Britain* (Mainstream, Edinburgh 1991)

Buxham, Tim. *Icehouses* (Shire Publication 1992, reprinted 1998)

David, Elizabeth. *Harvest of the Cold Months: The Social History of Ice and Ices* (Michael Joseph 1994)

Weir, Robin and Liddell, Caroline. *Ices The Definitive Guide* (Grub Street, London 1995, reprinted 1996, 1998)

Glossary

Bleeding The term used to describe the merging of flavours or syrups when making a layered iced dessert. To prevent this, smooth each additional layer of ice cream or sorbet and freeze until firm before adding the next, so that the layers of the finished ice cream appear well defined.

Cassata This is the name given to an Italian ice cream dessert, which is made with three different ice creams, set in layers in a round, bombe-shaped mould. The mould is sometimes lined with thinly sliced Madeira or Genoese sponge cake, or ready-made trifle sponges.

Dasher A plastic-coated paddle used in ice cream machines.

Float This American-style drink is made with cream soda or fizzy lemonade, fruit syrup and a scoop of vanilla ice cream.

Frappé Similar in texture to a granita, this snow-like iced drink can be made with fruit purée, fruit syrup or liqueur mixed with lots of crushed ice. The best remembered is the vibrant, green crème-de-menthe frappé.

Gelato This is the Italian word for ice cream. The style for a true Italian ice cream is lighter, with less cream and sugar, than American, English or French ice creams.

Granita An Italian water-based iced dessert that is beaten frequently during freezing to form grainy snow-like flakes of ice. Coffee granita is the classic version, but fruit flavours are also popular.

Knickerbocker glory This technicolour American sundae was quickly popularized in Britain and is made with scoops of vanilla ice cream and spoonfuls of different coloured jelly layered in tall sundae glasses, topped with whipped cream, strawberry sauce and sweets, then decorated with a wafer biscuit.

Kulfi This rich Indian ice cream is made by slowly boiling milk over several hours before flavouring with cardamom. It is traditionally frozen in small, conical-shaped moulds.

Neapolitan ice cream First sold in ice cream parlours and tea rooms in the 1850s, this ice cream is made of three contrasting colours of ice cream. It is set in a rectangular mould and served sliced. The most famous combination is chocolate, strawberry and vanilla ice creams.

Parfait This rich, creamy ice cream does not need to be beaten during freezing. It is made by whisking a hot sugar syrup into beaten egg yolks and, because the syrup is heated to the soft-ball stage, the finished ice cream has a wonderful texture even when served straight from the freezer. Parfait is usually set in individual serving dishes or moulds.

Popsicle The American name for an ice lolly, the very first of which was patented in America in 1923 as the Epsicle by Frank Epperson. The original Epsicle was flavoured with lemon.

Saccharometer This glass measuring device is used to check the sugar density of sorbet and ice cream mixtures. If there is too much sugar, the sorbet or ice cream will be too soft; too little and the sorbet or ice cream will have a hard, icy texture. It is used by

professionals and enthusiastic amateurs, but it is not essential unless you intend creating your own recipes or variations.

Semi-freddo This term is used for a semi-frozen Italian ice cream. The ice cream is mixed with crumbled biscuits, sponge cake or chopped candied fruit and set in containers or moulds. Semi-freddo is never beaten during freezing and is served when only just firm enough to scoop or slice.

Sherbet This is made in the same way as a sorbet, but with the addition of milk or cream. The term is most probably derived from the Arabic "Sharab", an early semi-frozen, sweet, milk-based drink.

Sorbet Classically made with sugar syrup and puréed fruit, this French water ice can also be made using wine or liqueurs. Sorbets are usually mixed with a little egg white to lighten the mixture.

Sorbetti This is the Italian word for sorbet.

Sundae This American iced dessert is served in rounded glass dishes generously filled with scoops of different coloured ice creams, then topped with fruit syrups or sauces, spoonfuls of cream and tiny sweets, grated chocolate or wafers.

Syrup All water-ice desserts are based on a simple sugar syrup, which is usually made with caster or granulated sugar. If making a large quantity of sorbet, prepare a large batch of syrup. It can be stored in the fridge in a covered container for 2–3 days or until required.

Water ice This is made like a sorbet but usually without the addition of eggs, although egg whites are sometimes added to improve the texture. Water ices were very popular in England during the Georgian and Victorian eras and were often flavoured with flowers, spices, fruits, wine and liqueurs.

Zester This useful, hand-held gadget is used to pare fine curls of rind from citrus fruits. It has four or five tiny metal holes that slice narrow strips of rind. Quick and easy to use, the citrus curls make a pretty finishing touch to even the most simple ice cream desserts and sorbets.

Acknowledgements

The author and publishers would like to thank Magimix and Gaggia for the kind loan of their ice cream machines. The author would like to extend her special thanks to Julie Beresford and Annabel Ford for their enthusiasm and help throughout photography and to her family for trying every ice cream that has appeared in this book.

Picture credits

The publishers would like to thank the following companies for their kind permission to reproduce their photographs: , p9 left and right, Charmet; p7 top right and centre, p11 top, p12 right, left, and bottom, p14 right and bottom, p15 top right, bottom right and centre, Hulton Getty; p7 top left, The Advertising Archives; p8 top and bottom, private collection, The Bridgeman Art Library; p10 left and right, p11 bottom, p13 top left, AKG.

Index

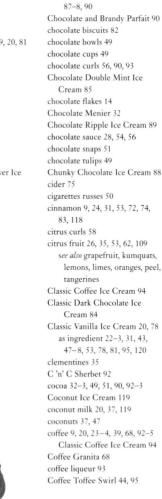

NOTES

NOTES

NOTES

NOTES